BUSHLAND STORIES

Please be sure to check these other great Australian books republished by Living Book Press-

NURI MASS
The Wonderland of Nature
The Little Grammar People
Australian Wildflower Fairies
Magic Australia

JOSEPH BOWES
The Aussie Crusaders

NORMAN LINDSAY
The Flyaway Highway

C.K. THOMPSON
Old Bob's Birds
Maggie the Magnificent
King of the Ranges
Red Emperor
Wild Canary
Tiger Cat
Monarch of the Western Skies
Thunderbolt the Falcon
Blackie the Brumbie
Warrigal the Warrior
Wombat
Willy Wagtail

This edition published 2019
By Living Book Press
www.livingbookpress.com

Copyright © Living Book Press, 2019

ISBN: 978-1-925729-21-4

All rights reserved. No part of this publication may be reproduced, stored in a retrieval system, or transmitted in any other form or means – electronic, mechanical, photocopying, recording or otherwise, without the prior permission of the copyright owner and the publisher or as provided by Australian law.

A catalogue record for this book is available from the National Library of Australia

BUSHLAND STORIES

AMY ELEANOR MACK

CONTENTS

THE WAVE	7
THE ANGLER	16
THE DISCONTENTED STREAM	27
THE BIRDS CONCERT	37
THE CHRISTMAS BELLS AND THE HOLLY BUSH	51
THE GREEDY SHAG	62
THE WHITE HERONS	72
THE TALE OF TIBBIE	82
THE BIRDS' ALPHABET	93
THE FLOWER FAIRIES	115
THE LION AND THE KANGAROO	122
THE THREE HEROES	134
THE BIRDS' CHRISTMAS TREE	141
THE LITTLE BLACK DUCK	156
THE PROPER WAY	167
THE LEAF THAT LONGED TO BE RED	175
THE STORY OF THE TURPENTINES	183
THE GALLANT GUM TREES	193

of the boat, was the prettiest sight she had ever seen. Three children were looking down at her, with their heads close together, their bright curls dancing in the breeze, and their faces shining with delight. They clapped their hands, and she tried to jump up to catch them. But she was not big enough to reach the top of the boat, so she danced along beside it.

"That's the prettiest Wave I've ever seen," said one child.

"Oh, I like the ones on the beach best," said another.

"Yes, the waves at Bondi are the prettiest in the world," said the third. Then they went on to talk of how the waves broke up on the beach at Bondi and washed round their feet when they paddled, and rolled them over on the sand when they bathed, and they all agreed that Bondi was the most beautiful place in the world, and they wished they could go back there.

The Wave listened to all they said, and she longed to see this wonderful Bondi of which they spoke, where the waves rolled the children over on the beach. She had enjoyed playing with the fishes and the birds, but now that she had seen these pretty pink and white children she had lost interest in her first playmates, and only wanted to play with children."

"Where do these children come from?" she asked the Wind.

"From that land over there," said the Wind.

She looked to where he was pointing, and saw, for the first time, a distant shore with green hills sloping down to the sea.

"Is that Bondi?" she asked eagerly.

"Oh, no; Bondi is a long way from here."

"How do you get there?"

"You must travel on and on for miles and miles. It is right across the ocean," replied the Wind.

"Have you ever been there?"

"Oh, yes; often."

"Did you like it?"

"Yes; I think it is one of the most beautiful places in the world. And I have such fun there, blowing the people's hats off and puffing their hair into their eyes. There are lovely waves there, too, and the children swim in them. Would you like to go there?"

"Oh, yes, yes," cried the Wave. "Could you take me?"

"Yes, if you would not grow tired on the way."

"Oh, no; I will not tire. Do take me, dear, dear Wind."

"Very well," said the Wind. "Let us start at once."

So off they went.

The Wind puffed out his cheeks till they looked as if they would burst, and blew upon the Wave to help her along. She lifted her foam-crowned head into the air, and raced along before him. Over the ocean they went at such a rate that even the sunbeams could scarcely keep up with them. Some wild sea eagles saw them and came rushing along to look, shouting "Go on, Wave, you'll win," for they thought it was a race. A crowd of porpoises heard the sea eagles, and also began to applaud, waving their fins wildly in the air as they rolled over. They looked so funny that the Wave could hardly run for laughing.

"Wait a minute, Wind," she cried, and she stopped running, and gurgled slowly past the fat porpoises, tickling them as they passed.

Then on they went again, rushing and tearing. They

passed many things on the way that the Wave had never seen before, although they were all old friends to the Wind. Big steamers came ploughing up the sea, frightening the Wave at first, till she found it was fun to slap up against them; big ships with white sails came gliding over the water, and she liked them better, and stayed to play around their bows, while the Wind whistled through their sails.

But the ships and steamers passed upon their way, and so the Wind and the Wave went travelling on again. Once they passed a boat like the one the children had been in, and the Wave danced up to look if there were any children there. But all she saw were two brown-faced fishermen, so she hurried past.

At last they came to an island, and as the Wave had never been close to land, they went to look at it. There were rough rocks all along the sea's edge, and a couple of men fishing.

"Where is the beach? Where are the children?" asked the Wave.

"There is no beach here, and no children—only grown-up men."

"Then we won't wait," said the Wave, "for I do not like the look of those rough rocks."

"You are right. Those rocks are rough, and would tear you to pieces if you went too near them."

"Then let us hurry past them," said the Wave; so they ran as hard as they could till the island and the rocks were left far behind.

But although they saw so many things that were new and strange, the Wave was not much interested in them. All she could think of was the long white beach at Bondi where she could roll the children over in her arms. Only that morning she had never heard of a beach or of children and she had been perfectly happy and contented; but now she knew that nothing would satisfy her but that beautiful beach of which those three children had talked.

"Is it very far now?" she asked the Wind, as the sun was beginning to travel down the western sky.

"No," replied the Wind. "We shall soon be there now."

They journeyed on again in silence for a little while; then the Wind said:

"Do you see that dark line at the edge of the sea?"

The Wave lifted her head, and looked across the water to where a long blue line rose into the air.

"Yes, I see," she said.

"That is Australia, and Bondi is straight before us. If we hurry we shall get there before sunset."

The Wave bubbled with excitement. "Sing to me, dear Wind," she said. So the Wind sang, and she danced along before him.

As they drew nearer, the blue line became more and more distinct, and they could see trees and cliffs, and long white lines between the cliffs.

"Those are the beaches," said the Wind, "and that long one with the low ground behind it is Bondi."

The Wave danced more quickly than ever.

"Oh, come on," she cried. "I can see children," and on they went.

The beach was quite near now, and they could see men and women walking along, and at the water's edge ever so many children playing, and the Wave saw that there were many other Waves now, all running up to the beach.

"Oh, the beautiful beach and the dear children!" she cried. "If only I can hold those children in my arms, and kiss that beach, I shall die happy. Help me, good Wind."

Then the Wind puffed out his cheeks wider than ever, and, bending low behind the Wave, blew hard and lifted her high. With arms outstretched and foam-hair flying, she raced along before him. In a minute she had reached the other Waves, all running to the shore but she ran fastest of all. Higher and higher the Wind lifted her, and she felt herself growing stronger. The weight of water below and behind seemed to be urging her forward; just in front she could see a group of children paddling, and behind them lay the beautiful shining white sand. She stretched out her arms still wider, lifted her head still higher, and with one leap reached the shore. Straight up she stood in a clear green wall, with a crest of white foam. For a second she seemed to stand still, then she hurled herself forward upon the group of children. Laughing and screaming, they tumbled along the sand beneath her, as she rolled them over with her arms. She wanted to wait and play with them, but she was moving too quickly to stop. On she went, up the white beach. Her heart was aching with joy. Tenderly and softly she kissed the sand as she passed, but each kiss seemed to leave her weaker, and as she reached the highest watermark the joy of lying on the dear beach was too much for her, and her heart broke.

Then slowly and gently the mother sea drew her back down the beach, till she was lost again in the deep blue ocean. And the Wind sighed sadly for the loss of his dear little companion, who had only lived for one short day.

THE ANGLER

AMONG THE rocks where the big green seaweeds waved their arms through the clear cool water, lived the Little Angler. He spent a solitary life lying on the yellow sand at the bottom of the bay, or swimming about under the shadow of the weeds. He never played with the other little fishes that sometimes came in shoals about the bay; he never jumped out of the water like the Mullet, or swam away into the open sea like the Bream. But he lived in the most retiring fashion imaginable, just as his parents had done before him.

One day as he was lying half asleep on the sand, a shoal of young Mullet came rushing past, all leaping and jumping and laughing as they hurried along. The Little Angler turned over to look at them as they passed above him. He was so like the sand in colour that the Mullet did not see him while he was lying still; but directly he moved, they caught sight of him, and shouted: "Hulloa, young sleepyhead. It's time you were out."

"Out where?" asked the Little Angler.

"Out at sea, of course," replied the Mullet. They had just come down from the lagoon, where they lived as babies, and thought themselves very fine and grown up because they could now swim in the deeper waters of the bay.

"But I never go to sea," said the Little Angler in surprise.

"Never go to sea!" echoed the Mullet all together. "Why, whatever do you do with your time?"

"I swim about amongst the nice, cool, green seaweed or lie on the soft sand at the bottom."

"Oh, how dreadfully slow," cried the Mullet, "and how tired of it you must get!"

"It isn't slow, I assure you. I like it very much and never grow tired of it."

"But do you mean to say that you never rush through the water and jump up to the top to have a look at the sky?"

"Certainly not," said the Little Angler with dignity. "I do not think it is at all nice for fish to jump out of the water. The shelter of the seaweed is the proper place for all well-behaved fish!"

"Oh, very well, lazy-bones," cried the Mullet, "if you like it you can have it. We prefer going to staying. Good-bye, old Stick-in-the-mud!" and with that they all rushed off again, jumping and splashing as they went.

The Little Angler gazed after them, admiring, in spite of himself, their speed and silvery brightness. As he watched them a strange feeling crept over him, and though he snuggled down again at once into the sand, he was not so happy and contented as he had been before the Mullet passed.

"Perhaps it is lazy to lie here so long," he thought after a while; " I think I shall go for a swim."

But though the water was cool and refreshing, and the seaweed as green as ever, he did not find the same pleasure in them as before, and his thoughts kept turning to the Mullet and the open sea.

He saw other fish going past, looking happy and bright as they swam away into the deeper water; but none of them stopped to speak to him. Indeed none of them saw him as he lurked in the shadow of the seaweeds. But he could see them, and he envied them their brightness, and for the first time in his life he felt lonely and dissatisfied.

"It's a shame that I should always have to stay here by myself instead of going away to the open sea, and having a lot of friends and plenty of fun," he grumbled to the Seaweed.

"Oh!" exclaimed the Seaweed, "is that what is the matter? I always thought you were a contented little fellow, and quite happy here with me. Haven't I been kind to you?"

"Yes," replied the Little Angler quickly, "you have always been very good to me, and I love you; but you never move from that rock, and you can't play with me."

The old Seaweed looked sad at these words, and answered slowly, "No, I am not much good at playing, I know, but I can hold you in my arms and shelter you from danger."

"But there's no danger here," protested the Little Angler, "and I want to go out into the world and see things instead of staying here all my life." The Seaweed saw that his little friend was thoroughly discontented and would never be satisfied again until he had found out for himself what the open water was like. As he was a very wise old weed he did not again try to hinder the Little Angler, and next day, when the little fish said he wanted to go and see the world, the Seaweed replied: "Then why don't you go?"

"I'm frightened to go by myself," confessed the fish. "I have no friends, and I don't know what I might meet out in that deep water. But, oh, I should just like to see what as he could: "Mr. Oyster, why am I too ugly to be seen?"

This aroused the Oyster, who opened his mouth and said crossly: "Go away, your noise annoys me."

"Stupid!" said a voice close by, "don't you know that a noise annoys an oyster?"

The Little Angler turned to the speaker and saw a Flathead.

"I was only asking him a polite question," he said very calmly, "but perhaps you could tell me instead?"

"Well, ask me and try," said the Flathead.

"Can you tell me why I am too ugly to be seen?"

"Pooh! that's an easy one," said the Flathead. "It's the shape of your head."

"What's the matter with my head?"

"Too fat. A flat head is beautiful, but a fat head is ugly. Now I'll ask you a question. What made the whiting white?"

"I don't know," said the Little Angler, bewildered by the Flathead's sudden change of subject.

"Because the Snapper tried to snap her!" said the Flathead, and off he swam.

"Oh dear, oh dear!" said the Little Angler, "how clever he is! I wish I could make jokes like that."

But although he admired the Flathead's cleverness, he wasn't satisfied with the reason he had given for his ugliness, so he thought he would ask someone else. As there was no one else about the rocks, he swam lower down, and there, lying on the sand below him, he saw a Sole. The Sole was an odd-looking flat fish, and, as the Little Angler looked at him, he thought to himself, "Well, I may be ugly, but I am glad I am not so ugly as that!"

However, he kept his thoughts to himself, and approaching the Sole said politely: "Please, Mr. Sole, can you tell me why I am too ugly to be seen?"

The Sole did not even bother to look at him before he answered: "For the Sole reason that you are not like me."

The Little Angler saw the joke, and exclaimed: "How clever you are!"

"Glad you think so," replied the other, and, closing his eye went to sleep.

The Little Angler waited for a few minutes, but as the Sole showed no signs of awakening to finish the conversation, he thought he would go somewhere else for his information; for, he said to himself: "The Sole is clever at making jokes, but he isn't truthful."

He had only gone a few yards when he heard a voice behind him say: "Well, Ugly, have you found out why you are so hideous?"

The voice sounded familiar, and he was not surprised, on turning round, to see the Parrot fish.

"No," he replied. "I have asked every fish I have met, and though they are all very clever at making jokes, they have not enough sense to answer my questions."

"Oh, oh, oh!" exclaimed the Parrot fish, "haven't enough sense, haven't they? Well I can answer your question without any trouble, for it's a very easy question indeed."

He laughed so loudly as he spoke, that he quite ruffled the water round him, and a swarm of young Prawns came swimming along to see what the fuss was.

"What's the matter?" they asked. "Why are you laughing so?"

"I am laughing at the small fish's question," replied the

Parrot fish. "He wants to know why he is too ugly to be seen. Can you tell him?"

The Prawns all turned to look at the Little Angler, and as soon as they saw him, began to giggle and point.

"Want to know why you are ugly, do you?" they shouted. "Well, we'll soon tell you."

"It's because you are hideous," said one.

"Look at your lip!" cried another.

"Look at your nose!" cried a third.

"And look at the whisker growing out of it!" shrieked a fourth, which sent them all off into fits of laughter.

As they spoke they all gathered round him, pointing at him with their long feelers, while the Parrot fish looked on and enjoyed the fun.

But it wasn't fun at all to the Little Angler. He thought it was very rude and unkind, as indeed it was. He wished he had never come into this deep water, and never met any of these rude fish. He thought of his kind old friend, the Seaweed, and longed for the shelter of his protecting arms. But the Seaweed was far away, and the horrid rude little Prawns were all around him, making insolent remarks. It was bad enough to have the big fish making fun of him, but to be teased and laughed at by such small fry was more than he could stand; and forgetting his fear of the Parrot fish, he shouted as loudly as he could:

"You all think you are very clever and very beautiful, but you are just rude and stupid and ugly, and I'm very glad I am not like you," and with that he turned and darted through the water as hard as he could go.

The Prawns and the Parrot fish were so astonished at this sudden outburst, that they could do nothing for a minute, and by the time they realized what had happened, the Little Angler was out of sight.

But, thinking that they were still chasing him, he kept on as fast as he could swim, till at last he came to his own part of the bay. There he saw his old friend waving to him.

"Whatever is the matter?" asked the Seaweed, for he could see no reason for the Little Angler's haste.

Breathless the Little Angler told his adventure, and the Seaweed listened silently. But when he burst into tears and sobbed, "Oh, why am I not beautiful and clever like other fish?" the kind old Seaweed folded his arms close round him, and said, soothingly: "There, there, my little one. Don't cry!"

"I didn't mind the big fish so much, but I couldn't bear those young Prawns making fun of me," said the Little Angler angrily.

The Seaweed was silent for a time before he answered. Then he said: "Would you like to punish the Prawns?"

"Yes, I would," said the Little Angler.

"They said you had a whisker on your nose, didn't they?"

"Yes."

"Then you can teach them the use of that whisker, for they are sure to come here teasing you since they have seen you. And you can show them that useful things are sometimes better than pretty ones."

"But it isn't useful," said the Little Angler.

"Isn't it? You just wait and see. Nature generally has some reason for a thing like that, and if it doesn't make you beautiful, it can certainly help you."

"How?" asked the Little Angler.

"Listen, and I'll tell you." And the Seaweed whispered

for a long time in the little fish's ear. What he said seemed to please his listener, for his face brightened and his tears vanished, and when the Seaweed had finished, the little fish looked as happy as ever.

The next morning, instead of going off again on his travels, he lay on the sand at the bottom of the bay, apparently asleep. And, although the Mullet came by and called out, "Hulloa, young Stick-in-the-mud, still asleep?" he took no notice, but lay still.

And after a while, as the Seaweed had predicted, the young Prawns came swimming along in a body. There were twice as many as there had been the day before, and they meant to have great fun with the Little Angler. They had heard of the Mullet's remark, and thought it very fine and clever, and as they came up they called out together: "Hulloa, young Stick-in-the-mud!"

The Little Angler answered not a word, but lay as still as if he were part of the sand.

The Prawns came closer. "He is stuck fast," said one.

"Stuck slow, I should think," said another, laughing.

But still the Little Angler made no reply. Then the Prawns came quite close, and growing very bold, jumped over his back, and pretended they thought he was a stone.

Then they made fun of his whisker, and asked each other what it was; while one, bolder than the others, pulled it.

Then a curious thing happened. Directly the Prawn touched the whisker the Little Angler's mouth opened, and shut with a snap, and the Prawn disappeared. It was done so quickly that the others did not see, and as there were so many of them, they did not notice the absence of one of their number. But they continued their jokes, and another went to tug at the whisker. Instantly he disappeared, just as the first had done. Still the others did not see, and the Little Angler lay as motionless as before.

One by one the Prawns came and tugged the whisker, and were snapped up by the Little Angler without the others noticing. Then the biggest Prawn went, and standing on the very lip of the fish, called out, "I am standing on a stone, and want to pull this whisker," and he gave a tug.

Immediately the fish's mouth opened, and snap went his jaws. But the Prawn was too big to disappear all at once, and the others saw what had happened.

Then began a commotion! They rushed away from the Little Angler, shrieking and screaming, for at last they realized that their brothers had been gradually disappearing, and they now understood the reason why. They did not wait to make any more fun of the Little Angler, but swam away for the deep water as hard as they could, and in a minute there wasn't one to be seen.

Then the Little Angler rose from the bottom, and went to tell his friend what had happened.

"I have had a very good breakfast," he said, "and I think the Prawns have had a very good lesson."

"Yes," agreed the Seaweed, "I think they have learned that it does not do to laugh at other people's appearance."

THE DISCONTENTED STREAM

ONCE UPON a time a little Stream lived in the beautiful brush country amongst the hills. His banks were bordered by all the brightest and greenest trees of the land; big coachwoods and maiden's-blushes spread their branches above his head; lillipillis with glossy-leaves and bright berries, and sassafras with starry blossoms bent over him, and were reflected in his mirror. Giant maiden-hair clustered close to his brink, and tree-ferns and bangalows whispered in the breeze and made his banks more beautiful. In the spring the birds built their nests in the bushes just above him, and he could watch the mother birds sitting on their eggs and the father birds bringing them food; and later on he could see the babies being taken out of the nest and taught to fly. In the summer the birds would come and bathe in his waters, and every evening they would come down to drink. There were satin-birds, thrushes, beautiful big blue pigeons with dull red crests, lovely little green pigeons, black magpies-in fact, all the shy, beautiful birds that live in the brush country.

And yet, with all this beauty round him, he was most discontented. He should have been the happiest stream in the world, for he had no worries or troubles, and nothing ugly to look at. But instead of singing happily as all good little streams do, he did nothing but murmur and mutter all day long. And the reason of his discontent was this:

Right in the centre of the gully along which he ran, there stood a steep, high hill, too high and steep for the Stream to cross over, and he had to turn out of his way and run round. At first he had not minded very much, for he thought he would be able to climb the hill when he grew bigger; but as day after day, and year after year went by, and he still had to run round the foot of the hill, he grew more and more sulky and discontented, until at last he hated the very sight of the hill.

"Great big ugly thing!" he said, as he ran past it, "why don't you stay up in the mountains instead of coming down into my gully?"

The hill took no notice of his remarks, but held his head high up, and did not even look at the Stream.

All up the hill-slope grew big gum-trees and young gum saplings. Here the bell-birds fed and called from dawn to dark, and never came down to feed among the trees at the Stream's edge. This also made the Stream angry.

"It isn't fair," he said, "that that old hill should have the bell-birds singing all day long, while I have only stupid, silent birds that are too shy to say a word. Why don't you sing?" he exclaimed angrily to a Wonga pigeon, who was drinking on the bank.

"Oh, oh, oh, I like that," said the Wonga. "Why don't you sing yourself, instead of grumbling all day? If you were brighter and happier we should not be so quiet."

"Stupid thing!" said the Stream to himself, "Of course he doesn't understand. He can fly away and get over the top of the hill whenever he likes. If I could only do that I shouldn't be as stupid and dull as he is. I should sing and dance with joy all day."

"Well, come and dance now!" shouted some Sunbeams, rushing down through the leaves of a big fig tree.

"I can't," said the Stream pettishly.

"Why can't you?" asked the Sunbeams.

"Because this place is too dull. If I could only get up to the top of that hill, I should be quite happy and bright, but this place is too dull for me to dance in."

"It's you that are dull," cried the Sunbeams, laughing at him. "Why don't you try to be happy?" Then they danced away amongst the trees calling out—"We'll come and see you again when you are in a brighter mood."

"It's all very well for them to talk," grumbled the Stream to himself, "they can dance away wherever they want to. They haven't got to run round that old hill all their lives. If they had to stay down here in the valley always they wouldn't laugh and dance like that," and he went grumbling on his way.

A little way along the gully he met a Lyre Bird, who came skipping down the hill and bent over to drink in the Stream's waters.

"Good day," he said in a cheerful voice, "isn't it a glorious morning?"

"H'm!" said the Stream sulkily, "it's not bad."

"Not bad?" echoed the Lyre Bird, "why, whatever more could you want? The weather is just perfect."

"Oh, yes, the weather's all right," grumbled the Stream, "but what's the good of that?"

"Why, it makes one feel so happy and cheerful. I want to sing and dance all the time when the weather is so good.

Don't you?"

"No," said the Stream crossly, "I don't."

"Whatever is the matter with you to-day?" asked the Lyre Bird. "Why are you so dull?"

"Dull," shouted the Stream angrily. "Everyone wants to know why I am dull. Well, I'll tell you why. I want to run up that hill, and I can't. There!"

"But Streams never run up hills!"

"I don't care what other Streams do. I know that I am tired of running round that hill all my life. I want to go up the slopes to the top, where the gum-trees and the bell-birds are."

"But," said the Lyre Bird, "there are prettier trees here, and more beautiful birds all along your banks."

"But they don't sing like the bell-birds. They are all so shy and stupid."

"I can sing to you as well as the bell-birds. Indeed I can mimic their notes if you like."

"Yes, but you are not here all the time," said the Stream. "You only stay for a little while and then you go back to the hills. Oh, those hills, they have all the best things!" and the Stream began to weep miserably.

The Lyre Bird felt very sorry for him. He was a kind-hearted bird, and he thought that it must be dull to stay in one place always. He could move from hilltop to valley just as he liked, and when he saw the Stream weeping, he pitied him and began to think what he could do to help him.

"Have you ever tried to climb the hill?" he asked.

"Yes, but I can never get up more than a few feet. I am not big or strong enough."

"Well," said the Lyre Bird, "I am very sorry indeed for

you, and I'll try to think of some way of helping you. I shall come back to-morrow and let you know if I succeed," and away he danced up the valley, singing cheerily as he went.

He had been so kind and sympathetic that the Stream felt quite brightened up, and was almost gay as he flowed along. There was something in the Lyre Bird's manner that gave him confidence, and he believed that he really might do something to help him up the hill. So he left off grumbling and almost began to sing. And when the birds came down to drink in the evening they all noticed that he was far less unhappy than usual.

"Have you been able to run up the hill?" asked the big blue Pigeon. "No," said the Stream, "but I think I soon shall. The Lyre Bird has promised to help me."

"Oh," said the Pigeon, "if he helps you, you'll be able to manage it, for he is so clever and can do anything he wants to."

"Can he?" said the Stream eagerly.

"Yes," agreed all the birds. "The Lyre Bird is a very clever fellow, and if anyone can help you he can." And then they all flew off to bed.

All through the night the Stream ran on, thinking of the morrow, and wondering what plan the Lyre Bird would suggest, and he felt so sure and happy that he began to sing a little gentle song, that lulled the birds on their branches, and made them sleep more peacefully.

Early in the morning, as the first sunbeams came stealing up over the hills, the Lyre Bird came dancing down to meet the Stream.

The Stream saw him in the distance, and called out, "Have you thought of anything?"

"Yes!" answered the Lyre Bird, and hurried towards him. "Yesterday when I left you," he said, "I went up into the hills, for I can think better there, and as I went along I suddenly thought I should go and ask the Waterfall if she knew of a way to help you. She was very kind, and listened while I told her your story, and she has promised to help you."

"How?" asked the Stream eagerly.

"When the next big rains come, she has promised to send all her children down to you. They will press you and push you and give you strength, so that you will be quite big and strong enough to go up the side of the hill instead of running round its foot."

"And when will the big rains come?" asked the Stream.

"The Waterfall says they are due now, and may come any day."

"Hurrah, hurrah!" shouted the Stream. "Thank you, thank you for helping me," and he ran gaily down the valley, singing loudly.

And the very next day the rains came. At first just a few odd drops fell, then faster and faster, and thicker and thicker they came, hundreds and thousands and millions of them, racing one another from sky to earth. They splashed down upon everything, on the leaves and the ferns and the Stream. The birds skulked amongst the bushes trying to find shelter from them, for they did not like the raindrops, but the stream spread his arms out wide, and loved to feel them falling upon him. He was so excited and happy, for he felt himself growing stronger every hour, and he thought that when the Waterfall sent her children he would be quite strong enough to climb the hill. So he sang so gladly that he did not notice that the bell-birds had stopped calling.

Then on the third day of the rain, the Waterfall sent her children as she had promised. With white hair flying they came rushing down the valley, dashing and splashing as they ran. The birds heard them, and those who had begun to build their nests on the low trees flew about crying, "The floods, the floods!"

But the Stream did not notice the birds' terror. He had eyes only for that shouting, noisy crowd of white-haired Wavelets.

"Hurrah, hurrah," he shouted. "Now I shall soon be able to climb the hill. Here are my friends!" And he lifted his head and rushed to meet them.

On they came with tremendous force, and before the Stream knew what was going to happen, they had dashed into him, and were swirling and swishing, and driving him along before them.

They swirled so hard that the Stream felt quite giddy, and called, "Oh, not so quickly, not so quickly, wait a minute!" But the Wavelets just laughed, and hurried on the harder, crying, "we can't wait. we're in a hurry to get to the hill."

The Stream had quite forgotten the hill in the shock, but at the Wavelets' words he remembered that they had come to help him climb it. So he said not another word about waiting, but hastened along with the others.

And in a very short time they came to the hill. There it stood, steep and straight, its gum-trees drenched with rain, and its bell-birds all silenced. But it held its head as proudly as ever up towards the sky, and took not the least notice of the Stream.

"Ah!" he cried, "soon you won't be so proud. Just wait

till I run over your stiff head, then you'll have to look at me. Come on!" he shouted to the Wavelets, and then they were right at the foot of the hill.

"Is this the place?" cried the Wavelets.

"Yes," shrieked the Stream, "this is the hateful hill that won't get out of my way."

"Then get ready, we are going to push," cried the Wavelets, and the next moment the Stream felt a tremendous push behind, and he was lifted gradually above his banks up the side of the hill.

The pushing hurt him terribly, and took his breath away, but he did not mind. "Push harder!" he cried; "lift me higher."

Then the Wavelets gathered all their force and, running underneath the Stream, they pushed till below him he could see the trees on his banks, half covered by water, and just above him were the saplings on the hill. He felt he was rising, but still the top of the hill was a long, long way up, and he could never reach it at this rate. Already he felt weakened by the pain of being pushed so hard, but he would endure anything to gain his end.

So he called as loudly as he could, "Oh, can't you push any harder?"

"Yes," shrieked the Wavelets, and with one terrific effort, they sent the Stream up, up, up, till he touched the trunk of the lowest sapling. Then just as he felt that at last he was going to have his wish, and run over the top of the hill, the Wavelets ceased pushing, weakened, and slipped from beneath him, and with a crash and a splash, the Stream fell back from the hill-side.

"Good-bye!" called the Wavelets, "we can't stay to help

you any longer, we are going home. You must climb the hill by yourself," and off they ran down the valley.

But the Stream did not answer them. The shock of falling back from the hill-side had quite stunned him, and he lay still and silent between his banks.

By this time the rain had ceased falling, and now the sunbeams began to creep down through the clouds, and soon the trees were sparkling in the light, and the birds began to twitter and call to each other that the flood was over.

But though all the world was smiling, the Stream lay silently in the valley, taking no notice of the birds or trees or sunbeams, till at last he heard his name called, and looking up, saw the Lyre Bird standing beside him.

"I didn't expect to find you here," said the Lyre Bird. "I thought you would have been far over the hill by now. I saw the Waterfall's children come rushing down, and I heard the birds saying there was a flood, and that you were rising up the hill. How is it that you are still here?"

"Oh!" moaned the Stream, "don't remind me of it. The wavelets were so rough. But here I am, and here I mean to stay."

"Do you mean that you don't want to go up the hill?" asked the Lyre Bird.

"Yes," said the Stream, "I shall be quite content in future to flow through the valley. I have found that hills are not meant for Streams to climb."

"You are quite right," agreed the Lyre Bird, "and I am so glad you have at last learned that. Now you will be contented and happy and sing as you go." Then he called out to the other birds, "Listen, all of you. The Stream is no longer discontented. He has learned that water won't run up a hill, and he's going to be happy and gay in the valley."

"Hooray, hooray!" shouted the birds in chorus. Then they all began to sing

> "Flow along the valley,
> Little Stream so gay,
> While the sunbeams golden
> Round about thee play.
>
> "Hill-sides steep and barren
> Were not meant for thee;
> Valley depths are better,
> All wise streams agree.
>
> "Flow then, happy Streamlet,
> Singing every day,
> Cheering with thy gladness,
> All things on thy way."

THE BIRDS CONCERT

THERE WAS a great commotion down in the gully. The birds were flying backwards and forwards among the palms and tree ferns. They were all chattering and twittering together, for it was the first day of Spring, which they were going to celebrate by a concert.

It had been rather a severe Winter, and the soft feeling of the Spring day was so delightful to the birds that they flew hither and thither, telling each other gaily "Spring is here, Spring is here."

They nearly all had bright new coats, having got rid of their old ones during the Winter, and as they all met together at the bottom of the gully where the concert was to be held, they made a beautiful picture.

The Emu was presiding; as he was the largest of the birds, he was always the chairman on occasions of this kind. He stood beneath a tall gum-tree, and in front of him was a clear space where the performers were to stand. On the other side of this space the birds sat in a circle. There were all kinds there, big and small, pretty and plain, and they all looked as happy as they could be, for birds dearly love the Spring.

The Emu stretched his long neck, and looked round with his big, bright eyes, to see that everyone was ready to begin; then he said:

"I think we should open with a chorus."

"Yes, yes, a chorus," shouted the birds, and then, all standing up together, they sang with all their heart, this Spring song—

"Spring is here! Spring is here!
And the skies are blue and clear.
Winter with its cold is past,
And the Summer's coming fast.

"Spring is here! Spring is here!
Flowers are opening everywhere.
New buds sprout upon the trees,
Butterflies float in the breeze.

"Spring is here! Spring is here!
Each bird calls unto his dear,
'Little mate, I love you best,
Come with me and build a nest.'"

It was a song they sang every Spring, and so they all knew it by heart, and sang it very well.

When they had finished, they went back to their places, and waited for the next item.

The Emu cleared his throat, and said: "I have not drawn up a regular programme, but I think the best singer should begin."

"Yes, yes, certainly," cried several birds.

"But, unfortunately," went on the Emu, "I am not able to decide who is the best singer. I myself do not profess to sing, but I know that several of you have very good voices, and I think the best way would be for us to decide now which is the finest singer, and then he can sing. I will give you three minutes to think it over, and then you can tell me which one you have chosen.

For three minutes after he had finished speaking there was not a sound except the whispering of the birds among themselves. Then the Emu said:

"Time's up!"

Immediately there broke forth such a noise and confusion that it sounded like some horrible fight. Every bird was calling out the name of the one it thought the best singer, and each name was different. There were cries of Reed Warbler, Jacky Winter, Butcher Bird, Bell Bird, Magpie, Lyre Bird, Native Canary, Tomtit, Wagtail, Cocktail, and a dozen other names.

"Order, order!" shrieked the Emu; "this will never do. I did not dream there would be so much difference of opinion. Clearly we must find some other way of deciding."

"Surely there is no need to decide. There can be no possible doubt about the matter; I am the best singer."

The speaker was the Lyre Bird, and he stalked into the centre with his long tail proudly lifted above his back.

"Indeed you're not the best singer," cried several birds angrily; "you're only a mimic."

The Lyre Bird just ignored them, and waved his tail scornfully as he said to the Emu, "Shall I begin?"

The Emu did not approve of the Lyre Bird's conceited manner, so he said: "No; I think we must prove which is the best singer by a competition. All those birds who have good voices must each sing a song, and the Parrot, the Cockatoo, and I shall decide which is the best."

"Why should the Parrot and the Cockatoo judge?" asked the Lyre Bird. "They can't sing."

"That is the reason why they will make good judges, for they will be unprejudiced."

"It seems to me a most foolish waste of time," went on the Lyre Bird, "for you must agree in the end that I am the best singer."

"I think your talking is the greatest waste of time," interrupted a Peewee. "Do be quiet and let us begin."

The Lyre Bird did not answer, but walked away with his tail raised in a most disdainful fashion.

"Let all those birds that are going to compete step into the front row," called the Emu.

Immediately about thirty birds hopped in front of the others, and stood in a row. They were of all sorts and sizes, some were large, some small, some brightly coloured, some plain brown, and they all looked very eager to begin.

"I think it would be best to commence with the smallest, and go on by turns to the biggest," said the Emu, "and each bird must step into the centre alone as he sings. Now let the smallest begin."

Instantly there stepped forward a small bird in a beautiful coat of black and blue, with a long tail raised above his back. It was the Blue Wren, or, as he is sometimes called, the Cocktail. He threw his head back and began to sing in a gushing voice:

"I'm a Cocktail, small and perky
And I hop with action jerky.
Tho' my song is small I fear,
It is very sweet to hear."

Before he had finished there was a rustling noise, and the Lyre Bird hurried up into the centre. He stood in front of the tiny Blue Wren, and lifting his head and tail in the same manner as the small bird, began to mimic him. He sang the same words in the same way, but his voice was richer and fuller, and it sounded as if there were several Blue Wrens singing in chorus.

The Blue Wren was most indignant, but the other birds couldn't help laughing, for it was such an absurd sight.

"No hope for you, young Cocktail," called out the Parrot, and the little bird hopped back to his place dejectedly.

The next bird to sing was the Silvereye, and he sang a sad little song in a very sweet, low voice, which sounded rather like that of a canary:

"A lonely little bird am I,
Whom people call the Silvereye.
I really wish I could be glad,
But as a rule I'm very sad.
Pee-ek, pee-e-ek, pee-e-ek."

"A very pretty little song, and nicely sung," said the Emu, but he was interrupted by the Lyre Bird, who in an exact imitation of the Silvereye, sang:

"A silly little bird are you,
And no one cares what you may do.
And tho' you pose as being shy,
I think you're really very sly.
Chee-ek, chee-ek, chee-ek!"

"Order, order," cried the Emu, "really, Lyre Bird, I am surprised at your bad manners. You ought to know better."

But the Lyre Bird only laughed scornfully and danced round the circle. "Don't take any notice of him," said the Cockatoo, "let us go on to the next."

"I'm the next," said a small bird who was known as the Native Canary, though his voice was not as much like a canary as was the Silvereye's. Still, it was very sweet and clear. He began on a high note, and his song went down like a musical scale, sounding like this:

```
Down,                    To
   down,                    like
      I                        my
         go                       song
            right                    you
               down                     can-
                  the                      not
                     scale.                   fail.
```

In a second the Lyre Bird had begun to imitate him, and he sang:

```
That                     As
   you                      vain
      are                       as
         vain                      an-
            we                        y
               plain-                    bird
                  ly                        could
                     see,                      be.
```

By this time the other birds had ceased to be amused and were all really annoyed. They began to complain to each other, saying that it was disgraceful, and that the Lyre Bird ought to be ashamed of himself.

"It's only because we're small that you mock us," shouted the Blue Wren. "You wouldn't dare to do so if we were big, you bully."

"He couldn't imitate us if he dared," said the Magpie, who was one of the biggest birds.

"Couldn't I?" sneered the Lyre Bird, "just wait and see."

The Parrot and the Cockatoo were talking excitedly to the Emu, as if they were making suggestions, and at last the Emu nodded his head in approval; then he said in a loud voice:

"As the judges, we have decided that the best singer shall be the one whom this rude Lyre Bird cannot imitate."

"That's a very good plan," said several of the birds, and so it was agreed, and the competition went on.

But though several birds sang entirely different songs in entirely different voices, the Lyre Bird mimicked them all. And the worst of it was that, although his voice was like the one he imitated, his tones were fuller than any of theirs. The Tomtit, Jacky Winter, Willy Wagtail, and Blackcap, having all sung and been mocked, retired in anger. Then there flew into the centre a slim, olive-brown bird. There was nothing very striking in his appearance, but when he began to sing, his first notes proclaimed him something out of the common.

He was a Reed Warbler, and this was his song:

"On the reeds of the creek do I swing,
As I sing, as I sing.
While the winds whistle soft in the grass,
As they pass, as they pass.

"And the waters wash softly and sweet
At my feet, at my feet.
No bird is more joyful than I
'Neath the sky, 'neath the sky.

"But I'm not only happy and gay
In the day, in the day,
For I sing with a wondrous delight
All the night, all the night."

He sang with a clear, sweet, thrilling voice, which delighted every ear. As he finished, there was a burst of applause from his listeners.

"Surely the Lyre Bird will not try to imitate that," said the Magpie. But he did not know the limits of the Lyre Bird's impudence, for as soon as the applause had died away, the mimic began. He could not remember all the words of the Reed Warbler's song, so he whistled the air in the very same way. But this time the imitation was not better than the original; indeed, it was scarcely as good. Still it was an imitation, and so it could not be said that the Reed Warbler had won the competition.

Then there flew down two very beautiful birds. One had a glorious yellow breast, with a black collar and head, and a white throat. The other was just the same, except that his breast was red instead of yellow. They were both

Thickheads, or Thunder Birds, and two of the most beautiful of all the birds. Side by side they stood, and in rich, round voices they sang:

"In open scrub or thickest brush,
We may be found;
And into song we always rush
At any sound.

"Report of gun or thunder heard
Brings forth our song;
And so we're known as Thunderbird,
E-cheu, e-chong!"

Their voices were even more clear and loud than the Reed Warbler's, though they could not sing so long; and the last two words, "E-cheu, e-chong," were sung in a queer way which sounded very like the cracking of a whip.

But though their song was beautiful, sad to say it was very easy to imitate, and the Lyre Bird danced up and down saying "e-cheu, e-chong," over and over again.

Still the birds did not despair, and one after another they sang. Each one came up hoping the Lyre Bird could not imitate him, and each one went back disappointed and angry, as he heard his music mocked. At last there were only three song birds left to sing—The Bell Bird, the Butcher Bird, and the Magpie. The Bell Bird's song was this:

"Ding, dong, ding, dong!
Listen to the Bell Birds song.
You can hear it far and near,

Ringing out so loud and clear,
Dig, ding, ding."

This the Lyre Bird mimicked with the greatest ease. Then the Butcher Bird sang his song:

"They call me Butcher Bird,
A name which suits me well;
For little birds I chase and kill
And carry off within my bill,
As anyone can tell."

And again the Lyre Bird mimicked.

"Only one more," said the Emu. "Surely, Magpie, you can sing something too hard for this impudent fellow to copy."

"I'll try," said the Magpie, and in a deep, rich contralto voice, he sang:

"Quite early in the morning I awake,
And pour my song out to the coming day.
Across the paddocks you can hear my voice,
Gurgling and gay."

But, alas, though his voice was quite unlike that of any of the other birds, it was just as easy for the Lyre Bird to imitate. He did so, running up and down with his tail spread high, and rejoicing to see the Magpie's dismay.

"Ah, ah, so you thought I could not imitate you, Mister Magpie," he cried. "Your song was to be too good for me to copy. Listen to this," and in a deep contralto voice, just like the Magpie's, he sang:

"The Magpie is a very cunning fowl,
Who gets up early—so you've heard him say,
And eats the food of all the other birds,
While they're away.

"How do you like that, Mister Magpie?"

"Shame, shame!" cried several birds, for the Magpie himself was too angry to speak. But the Lyre Bird ignored them, and turning to the Emu, said:

"Now, Mister President, I think you must admit that I am the best singer."

Before the Emu could answer, the Parrot said quickly: "But there are still plenty of birds you haven't imitated. Let them compete."

"Yes," said the Emu, "the true songsters have all sung and been mimicked; now let the other birds try."

"Oh, very well," replied the Lyre Bird, "I have no objection, though it is a terrible waste of time."

"However, it shall be done," said the Emu sternly. So the other birds, who do not profess to sing, came and made songs. There were Parrots, Cockatoos, Catbirds, Peewees, Black Magpies, Woodpeckers, and many others. Many of them just gave several loud shrieks, which the Lyre Bird immediately echoed. But the Black Magpie sang a real song. In a loud clanging voice he shouted:

"Come-along, come-along, come-along!
Come-along, Mister Lyre Bird, and try,
If, without going wrong, you can mimic the song
Of the wonderful Black Magpie.
Come-along, come-along!"

"Pooh! do you really believe I can't imitate that?" and the Lyre Bird at once began to shriek:

"Get-along, get-along, get-along!
Do you really believe I need try
To mimic your song? Why an old broken gong
Could mimic the Black Magpie.
Get-along, get-along."

The Black Magpie was the last. All the birds had sung-big and little, young and old, those with voices, those with none-and the Lyre Bird had mocked them all. They all looked very miserable, and not a bit like the same happy birds that had sung their spring chorus. The Emu looked worried, the Parrot and the Cockatoo looked very cross, and the only one that looked happy was the Lyre Bird. With mincing steps he danced round the circle, bowing mockingly to each bird as he passed. Then he stopped before the Emu, and said in a most conceited voice:

"Surely you are satisfied now that I am the best singer. Not one of those stupid birds can sing a song that I cannot copy. Whether they sing or shriek, I can mimic them all."

"Not quite all," said a voice overhead. Everyone looked up, and there on a branch sat the Kookaburra, whom everyone had forgotten. "You haven't mimicked me yet," said the Kookaburra.

"You didn't sing," objected the Lyre Bird.

"No, I have been enjoying the fun, and it has amused me so much that I can now laugh heartily. Will you try to copy me, Lyre Bird?"

"Of course I can copy you. There is no need to try."

"Very well. Listen carefully;" and Kookaburra threw his funny long bill into the air, and began:

"A laughing Jack am I.
Ha-ha, ha-ha, ha-ha!
I laugh away, I laugh all day,
I laugh both low and high.
Ha-ha, ha-ha, ha-ha, ha-ha, ha-ha-ha,
Ha-ha-hah!"

As he began to sing in his queer laughing gurgle, the Lyre Bird's face lost its mocking smile, and became very long, and the longer the Kookaburra laughed, the longer the Lyre Bird's face grew, till finally it was as long as his tail.

At last the Kookaburra stopped, and the other birds all cried out:

"Mimic that, copy-cat, if you can!"

The Lyre Bird felt far from laughing, but he began his imitation of the Kookaburra. "Ha, ha, ha, ha."

He could get no further. Though he stretched his throat to the utmost, and strained his lungs, he could not make a laugh like the Kookaburra's. Again and again he tried, but in vain. He could not get beyond the first two notes.

Then all the other birds shouted and screeched with joy, and the Kookaburra cried:

"Ah, Mister Lyre Bird, who's the best singer now?" and then he burst out laughing again.

But this was too much for the Lyre Bird. He could not bear to be laughed at, although he had made such fun of the others, so he just turned his back, and ran away as fast as his legs could carry him.

And to this day you will never find the Lyre Bird with other birds. He plays only with his own brothers; and in the deep gullies you will often hear him mimicking all the birds in the bush, except the Kookaburra; for even yet he can only copy the first few notes of that strange laugh.

When he had gone the Kookaburra said:

"I suppose I have won the competition, although as you all know I can't sing a note. So I propose, Mister President, we do not bother about who is the best singer, but let us finish up with a general chorus."

So they all sang together:

"We're all very happy little birds,
And it doesn't matter who sings best,
The Lyre Bird's away,
But he's wasted all the day,
And the sun now is sinking in the west.

"So no matter who may sing the finest song,
To do our best the whole of us will try.
If the music of our voice
Makes a single heart rejoice,
We'll be satisfied; and now we say 'good-bye.'"

THE CHRISTMAS BELLS AND THE HOLLY BUSH

THERE WAS one thing in the garden which the House Mother loved better than anything else, and that was the Holly Tree. She had brought it from England with her when it was a small plant in a pot, and she was quite a young girl. Now the Holly was a big tree and she was an old woman.

There were plenty of other trees and flowers in the garden, many of them far more beautiful than the Holly, but though the House Mother took great care of them all she gave extra attention and love to the Holly. If she had known what a very disagreeable tree it was, she never would have been so fond of it. But she saw in it all the beauty and happiness of her old home, and was blind to the fact that it was really a very proud, bad-tempered bush.

But though she was not aware of the Holly's faults, all the other flowers and trees in the garden were. They knew that it was the proudest and nastiest tree amongst them, and instead of being sweetened by the love the House Mother spent on it, it was only vain and arrogant. And it was so ungrateful that it would even prick her fingers if it noticed her paying attention to any other plant.

"You ought to be ashamed of yourself," said the Rose indignantly, when one day the Holly pricked the House

Mother's finger so deeply that it bled. "How can you be so ungrateful?"

"Pooh!" said the Holly, "Why should I he grateful, I should like to know? She should be grateful to me for living in her garden."

"Oh!" exclaimed the Rose in horrified surprise.

"Do you forget all that she has done for you all your life?"

"I don't see that she has done anything much, and she knows that I wouldn't stay here if she didn't please me."

"And what about the love she has always given you?"

"Oh, well, how can she help loving me when I am so beautiful?" And the Holly held his stiff head up higher than ever, and looked very ugly and conceited.

"How can she help loving you?" echoed the Rose, "I'll tell you how. Because you are vain and ungrateful and cruel, and do not deserve her love."

The Holly laughed affectedly as he answered "The House Mother evidently doesn't agree with you. She sees that I am the most exquisite tree in her garden, and so of course, she loves me."

"Not at all, not at all," said a Red Gum, that bent over the fence from the paddock outside. "The reason the House Mother loves you is not because you are beautiful, but because you remind her of her childhood and her old home, and the little cottage garden from which she brought you."

"What do you mean?" asked the Holly, indignantly turning towards the Red Gum. "I come from no cottage garden. I come from a noble line, and can trace my ancestors back for centuries."

"Perhaps so!" said the Red Gum, "but we are not speaking of your ancestors. I say that you came from a cottage garden, and your manners prove your want of breeding," and with that he waved back over the fence, and took no more notice of the Holly.

Instead of profiting by the Red Gum's remark, and making up his mind to improve his manners, the Holly grew ruder and crosser each day, till the other flowers almost hated him. He hadn't a nice word for anyone. He snubbed the little plants unmercifully and called them weeds and intruders; he was impudent to the big trees and called them upstarts; and the beautiful flowers, the roses, carnations, and stocks, he insulted most of all, for they were out in all their spring glory, and were admired and beloved by everyone.

Still the House Mother loved him and petted him, for even the wisest House Mothers cannot see into a tree's heart, and she did not know of the hatred and ill-feeling that was rife in her beautiful garden.

As the spring passed on into summer, the blossoms of the fairest flowers drooped and died, one by one, till there wasn't a single bloom left on rose, carnation or stock. The Holly rejoiced to see the blossoms fade, for, as is the way with all jealous and discontented people, he could not bear to see beauty in anyone but himself. And when the last blooms died and disappeared, he became almost good tempered.

"Now," he said, in a loud conceited voice, "I think you must all agree that I am the most beautiful thing in the garden. And when Christmas day comes, you will know that I am certainly the most important."

"Why should we know it especially on Christmas day?" asked a wild Clematis, who had only lately come to the garden, and did not know much about the garden flowers.

The Holly looked at her with pitying contempt. "Of course one must expect ignorance in such weeds as you, but as you ask me, I will tell you why I am most important on Christmas day. On that day all the flowers are dead, but I am in my full beauty, and people make songs about me, and pick great bunches of my scarlet berries to decorate their houses and churches."

"Your berries!" said the Clematis, "Where are they? I can only see dull green leaves on you."

The Holly looked at her disdainfully, but before he could think of what to say, there came a laugh from across the fence, and the Red Gum bent over.

"Ho, ho, friend Holly," he said. "So you are remembering the old world and the cottage garden now?"

"What do you mean?" demanded the Holly, who rather dreaded the Red Gum's satire.

"You were surely thinking of them just now when you explained to the Clematis why you were so important on Christmas day. For though that may be quite true of your family in the old world, it is not at all the same here."

"Why is it not the same? Doesn't the House Mother pick a piece of me every Christmas to put on her plum-pudding?"

"Yes, but that is simply because she used to do so when she was a girl. We all know that the House Mother loves you, but we have never seen anyone else pick the red berries you speak of to decorate their houses."

The Holly looked foolish and uncomfortable at these words, but did not answer, for he knew that they were true.

"You live too much in the past, my friend," went on the

Red Gum, "and you imagine that things are the same here as they were in your youth across the world. But they are not. At Christmas time in England when the snow is on the ground and all the other flowers are asleep, people are very glad to have your scarlet berries. But things are different in this land. There are plenty of flowers in bloom for Christmas day, and you have not a single berry on you. No one cares anything about you except a few old fashioned people like the House Mother, whom you remind of their youth. All true Australians prefer their own Christmas flowers, and do not bother about you."

"What Christmas flowers have they?" asked the Holly, who had never been outside the garden and knew none of the bush blossoms.

"Christmas Bush and Christmas Bells, of course," replied the Red Gum.

"I never heard of them," said the Holly with contempt.

"Never heard of them," echoed the Clematis; "why, I thought you were so clever that you knew everything. And you have never even heard of the beautiful Christmas Bush and Bells, which are far more lovely than you."

"Well, you will soon have a chance of seeing the Christmas Bells," said the Red Gum, "for there is a family of them growing beneath my shade, just outside the fence, and they will be in full bloom within the month."

The Red Gum's words were true. In a week the Christmas Bells began to come through the ground, first one little spear, then another; till in a short time there was a group of bright red bells waving in the breeze.

All the trees in the garden admired them, and soon grew to love them, for they were so bright and merry and full of fun. All except the Holly. He had to admit to himself that their red bells were far more beautiful than his own dull green leaves, but this only made him dislike them more than ever.

"Noisy vulgar upstarts!" he said with a sneer when the Bells rang cheerfully, and he never lost a chance to say something unkind about them. He was nastier to them than he had been to all the others put together, for he hated them worst of all.

The Christmas Bells could not understand him. They were loving, happy little flowers, with kind words for everyone, and at first they tried to make friends with the Holly. But he treated all their advances so cruelly, that they were hurt, and did not dare to approach him. And their pretty heads hung sadly when they heard his unkind remarks about them. Still they never returned his nastiness, and never spoke an unkind word about him.

As the end of the year grew near the weather grew hotter and hotter. A furious blast of scorching wind blew from the west, drying up everything on its way. The tender leaves of the garden plants shrivelled and died, and the plants themselves began to droop and pine away. The Holly felt it most of all. It was the hottest summer he had ever known in his life, and he longed for the snow and cold wind of his youth. The House Mother did all she could for him, but water was scarce, and she could spare very little. Each day he grew fainter. He did not take it quietly as did the other flowers, but grumbled the whole day long, and by his bad temper exhausted what strength he had left, so that when Christmas Eve arrived he was really very ill and weak.

"I wish I had never come to this hateful country," he cried. "It is not fit for decent trees to live in."

"It's quite fit for the trees that belong to it," answered the Red Gum, who was not troubled by the heat.

"Oh, of course it's good enough for coarse uncultured things like you," retorted the Holly.

"It's a pity you came here," replied the Red Gum.

"Yes, it is," wailed the Holly, and he began to moan miserably.

"Oh, don't be unkind to him, Red Gum!" cried the Christmas Bells, the only flowers left alive.

"He deserves it," grumbled the Reel Gum. "He has always run down our land."

"Yes, but he is ill now."

"I don't care. I hope the wind will kill him," said the Red Gum savagely.

"Oh, Red Gum, Red Gum," cried the Bells. "We are shocked at you."

"Well, I don't exactly hope it will kill him, but I hope it will teach him a lesson," admitted the Red Gum.

Here they were interrupted by a deep moan from the Holly, who was now past speech. He looked so weak and pitiful that the Red Gum's heart softened towards him, and when the Bells cried, "Oh, Red Gum, lend him your shade, that will help him!" he did not answer, but bent across the fence, and threw his shadow over the Holly, protecting him from the sun.

The Holly opened his eyes and looked up, and the Bells and Red Gum saw something in his glance that had never been there before. It was a look of gratitude.

Instantly the Christmas Bells forgot the past. All they

thought of was that here was a fellow plant dying for want of help. They put their heads together, and asked—"What can we do? What can we do? We must save him."

"Nothing can save him now but the Storm Fairy," said the Red Gum.

"Where is the Storm Fairy?" asked the Bells in one voice.

"Miles away, down by the sea."

"Couldn't you call to him to come?"

"He wouldn't hear me."

"Would he hear if we all rang our loudest?" asked the biggest Christmas Bell.

"Yes, he might hear that," said the Red Gum.

"Then do let us try!" called the Bells. And they began to ring. "Ding-a-ding, ding-a-ding, ding, ding, ding!" they went, growing louder at each peal. Their music travelled above the noise of the Westerly Wind, across the plains, through the bush, over the mountains, to the coast, till at last it reached the sea where the Storm Fairy was.

The Storm Fairy heard it, and wondered what it was. As it grew more and more persistent, he determined to go and find out. So he started off towards it. Across the mountains he went, through the bush, till he came to the plains. The farther he travelled the louder the ringing grew, and at last he realized that it was someone ringing for help.

"I suppose that Westerly Wind has been up to his games again," he said to himself. "I must hurry along and prevent him doing too much mischief."

So he hurried onwards with a rush and a roar towards the garden.

The Red Gum saw him in the distance, and told the Bells.

"Don't stop ringing," he said, for they were growing

very tired. "Don't stop, or he may pass by and not know we need him."

So the Bells swung themselves backwards and forwards with a fresh effort, although they were now so tired they could scarcely move. But they glanced at the drooping Holly, and determined to do their utmost.

The Storm Fairy stopped in the distance to listen; heard the fresh effort of the Christmas Bells; found where it came from and started off towards it. With a rush and a roar he came, accompanied by a train of black clouds. Half way across the plain, he met the Westerly Wind.

"I will teach you to behave!" he cried, and hurled a thunderbolt at him. The Westerly Wind did not wait to fight, but turned and fled far away across the land. And the Storm Fairy went on his way.

"I'm coming, I'm coming," he shouted as the Bells sent out a fresh peal, and the next minute he had reached them.

He saw at a glance what had happened; saw the shrivelled garden, and the insensible Holly in the centre; and he saw the Christmas Bells outside the fence, now still and exhausted after their exertion.

"That Westerly Wind has been having a fine game," he said. "It looks as if I were only just in time. But I can save you all."

He gave a loud shout which shook the sky, and immediately the rain began to fall. Down it came, first in drops, then thicker and thicker, till the whole country was hidden in a sheet of falling water. All through the night it fell, soaking into the parched earth, and bringing fresh life to the plants. One by one they revived and lifted their heads, and stretched out their arms to drink in all they could.

When the morning came the Storm Fairy had passed on, but he had left a soft, cool, moist breeze behind him, and the garden rejoiced.

Before the sun was up very high, the House Mother came out to see how her dear plants were. With her came her little grand-daughter, who clapped her hands and ran about from plant to plant, wishing them all a merry Christmas. For it was Christmas day.

"I must pick a piece of Holly for the pudding," said the House Mother, going towards her favourite.

But the little girl had caught sight of the Christmas Bells outside, and ran towards them crying, "Oh, here are some lovely Christmas Bells. Let us have them for the pudding, Granny."

The House Mother looked over the fence, and saw the red Bells swinging happily to and fro, without a trace of the hard work they had done the day before.

"They are very beautiful," she said, "and perhaps we should have them. As this is your first Christmas with me, dear, and you are a little Australian, we shall have a real Australian Christmas," and with these words she walked away from the Holly, and over to where the Christmas Bells were growing.

The other plants all looked at the Holly, expecting to see him very angry. But instead, to their surprise, a sweet smile was on his face, and he nodded pleasantly towards them.

"She is quite right," he said. "The Christmas Bells are the best and bravest of us all, and they deserve the place of honour. I know I have been vain and unbearable to you all, and most unkind to them, but they have taught me many things by their forgiveness, and I am glad that they are to take my place to-day, and I am proud to call them cousins!"

"Hurrah!" cried the Red Gum, as the Holly finished speaking. "That's the way for an English tree to talk, and I am proud to call you cousin," and he leaned down over the fence and gave the Holly a friendly kiss.

And the Christmas Bells rang with happiness, for by their love they had brought peace and goodwill into the garden.

THE GREEDY SHAG

THE BIG Shag sat on a fence beside the lagoon, looking very proud and pleased with himself. He was a handsome bird, with a nice black and white coat, but it was not of his appearance that he was thinking. He was the biggest shag in the district, and the greediest, and he was looking pleased because he had his feeding-place all to himself.

The lagoon where he lived was a popular place for shags, and they used to meet there to fish for their dinners. But this morning none of the others had arrived, and the Big Shag thought he would have a good day's fishing all alone. On the other side of the lagoon some sandpipers were running about, and out towards the sea a couple of gulls were circling overhead, but the Big Shag did not mind them, for they were not likely to disturb him.

"I am very glad none of my brothers and cousins are here to-day," he said to himself. "They do get in the way so, and frighten the fish, and then I cannot catch enough. But I'll have a good feast to-day," and he clicked his beak greedily.

He had hardly finished speaking when he heard a swishing, whistling noise, and a whole flock of shags came flying towards the lagoon. There were four kinds of them, the big black and the little black, and the big black and white, and the little black and white. They flew straight to the lagoon, and settled in the trees just beside the Big Shag. He looked round at them angrily, and said—

"What do you want?"

"We're a bit late," said one of the black shags, "but we've been playing down on the beach."

"It's a pity you came at all," answered the Big Shag. "Nobody wanted you."

The shags on the tree all looked at each other in surprise.

"Well, that's pretty cool," said the Black Shag who had spoken before. "Anyone would think you owned the lagoon."

"So I did before you youngsters came. I am the eldest, and lived here long before any of you. It is only because I am so kind that I have let you come here to fish; but now that you are so impudent, I won't allow you to stay."

"How are you going to stop us?" asked the Black Shag.

"I'll soon show you," said the Big Shag; and, rising quickly, he darted to the tree.

The birds in the tree flew up quickly to get out of his way, for they all knew how strong he was. But one little black shag was too slow and the Big Shag knocked him over on to the ground, where he lay stunned.

"Shame, shame, you coward!" cried several of the birds.

The Big Shag took no notice of them, but rushed at some other small birds who had taken shelter in the next tree. They did not wait, but flew away as fast as they could. Then he turned to drive away the others, but, to his anger, they had all flown down to the lagoon, and were busy catching their breakfasts.

He swooped down after them, calling, "Come out of my

lagoon," but instead of answering him, the others straightway dived into the water after fish.

This made the Big Shag very angry indeed, but he did not see how he could drive them away. For he was such a coward that he was afraid to chase them as he had the little ones. So he just mumbled to himself—

"Oh, well, I'll see that they don't take my fish. I'll eat them all myself," and, so saying, he dived into the water after a fish that was passing by.

I must tell you that shags do not dive from a height, as terns and divers and gannets do, but they swim along on the surface of the water and wait till they see a fish, then they plunge in and swim along underneath the surface of the water for quite a long way.

Now the Big Shag was very strong, and he could stay under the water a long time; he thus caught a great many fish, and every one he got he gobbled greedily, as if he had had nothing to eat for a week. Whenever he came to the surface, if he saw another bird near him, he would fly at it with outstretched beak and drive it away. Sometimes he would attack his companions from underneath, when they could not see him, till at last they grew tired of dodging him, and, as they had all had as much breakfast as they wanted, they flew away and left him to himself.

"The Big Shag was in a bad temper to-day," said one of the birds, as they flew across the sand.

"Yes," said the Black Shag, "he was very cross, but I expect he'll be better to-morrow."

"I don't think I'll go to the lagoon again," said one bird who was timid. But the Black Shag said "Oh, you must not mind him. He'll behave better to-morrow."

But the Black Shag was mistaken, for when they flew down to the lagoon on the following day, the Big Shag was more angry and nasty then ever, and chased every bird that came near the water, till, at last, as they could not fish in peace, they all flew away, leaving the Big Shag to himself.

Then the Big Shag felt quite happy, for he thought to himself, greedily—

"Now I can eat all the fish in the lagoon."

So he fished all day, and ate fish after fish, and the more he ate the more he wanted, for he was as greedy as greedy could be.

The poor fish were dreadfully worried. It was bad enough when the birds fished for their meals because they were hungry, but to have this big bird chasing them the whole day long was terrible. They had no peace at all. And the worst of it was that there was no chance for them to punish the Big Shag, for, if they attempted to go near him, he just gobbled them up. They were mostly Flathead and Mullet, which are nice narrow fish, and easy for the Shag to swallow in one gulp, so that they had no chance of escaping when he caught them.

All the fishes met in a corner of the lagoon to talk the matter over.

"This can't go on," said Mrs. Mullet. "I am getting quite thin, rushing away from that monster; and as for the children, they are worn to shadows."

"But what are we to do?" asked someone.

"Suppose we leave the lagoon and go out to sea. He won't follow us there," suggested old Mister Flathead.

"That's all very well for us grown-ups, but we can't take the children out into the rough water, and if we leave them behind the Shag will eat them," said Mrs. Mullet.

"I wish the old Shag would choke when he is swallowing one of us," said a young flathead, angrily. "But we're too thin and small to stick in his throat. It's a pity we're not as broad as the bream."

As he spoke, Mrs. Mullet turned and looked inquiringly at old Mister Flathead; then she said slowly—

"That's not a bad idea."

"Could we manage it?" asked old Mister Flathead.

"Manage what?" asked the young flathead. "Whatever are you two talking about?"

"Don't ask questions," replied Mrs. Mullet. "You'll understand later on."

Then she and old Mr. Flathead and several of the older fish swam off together, all talking mysteriously as they went.

The young fish stayed where they were, for they were afraid to venture forth alone, and they watched their elders swim right away to the other end of the lagoon.

"I believe they're going out to sea, and going to leave us alone," said one little fish, beginning to cry.

"Oh, no; they wouldn't be so mean," said the young flathead. But he did not feel quite so sure in his own mind when a couple of hours passed and there was no sign of the elders.

The little fish were getting very frightened. They could hear the Big Shag swimming about in the water, and they all huddled together under the reeds. The Big Shag was very angry, because he could find nothing to eat, and they heard him grumbling and growling, and saying that he would eat them all when he caught them. Then they huddled together closer than ever.

At last they heard a faint noise in the distance, and the young flathead peeped out from the reeds to see what it was.

"Here they come!" he said joyfully; and in a few minutes the elders were back again.

But they were not alone. Behind them, looking very excited, were seven young bream.

Mrs. Mullet introduced them to her family and to the young flathead, saying—

"These fine young bream have come to stay with us for a while, and I hope you'll be friends with them, my dear."

The young flathead said, "How do you do?" and the little mullet bobbed their heads. But the young bream just waved their fins in a condescending manner, and went poking about in the reeds.

"Why did you bring them here?" the young flathead asked Mrs. Mullet. But she only answered—

"Just wait, and you will see."

And they were to see very soon.

The bream were very vain young fish, and looked down on the mullet and flathead, and would not condescend to take any notice at all of the children. So when Mrs. Mullet said to them—

"I wonder whether you can swim as fast as the young flathead?" they laughed scornfully, and one replied—

"We wouldn't be much if we couldn't."

"Well, I'm not so sure," said Mrs. Mullet, "for the flathead is a pretty fast swimmer."

The bream laughed again, and said rudely—

"Do you really believe that we can't swim faster than that ugly flathead fellow? Well, we'll soon show you. Let him try to race us."

"Very well," said Mrs. Mullet, for this was exactly what she wanted. "You can race, and I'll judge which is the quicker."

"Right!" said the bream. "How far shall we go?"

Mrs. Mullet looked round thoughtfully, as if measuring the distance. In reality she was looking to see where the Big Shag was, but the bream didn't know that. She saw him in the middle of the lagoon, near some rushes, and he looked very angry. So she said to the bream—

"You see that clump of rushes?"

"Yes."

"Do you think you could swim as far as that?"

The bream burst out laughing, and said, "Why, we could get there and back before you could turn round," and without waiting for another word, they all darted off towards the rushes.

They were so vain of their speed that they did not notice anything round about them. Straight for the rushes they swam, and the mullet and flathead watched them from the distance. The bream knew they were being watched, and they swam their hardest just to show off. They were too intent on themselves to notice a black and white figure swimming quickly towards them from one side. All they thought of was how quickly they could reach the rushes. They were just a few yards off, and the biggest of all was leading. In a second they would be right amongst the rushes.

"I guess we've rather surprised old Mother Mullet," said the leader. But before he could say another word—swish, swish, came the black and white figure, and he was fast in the beak of the Big Shag.

"A shag, a shag!" cried the others, and without waiting to see what became of their companion, they all swam off to the ocean as hard as they could.

In the meantime, the mullet and flathead were watching excitedly. They saw the Big Shag swimming towards the bream, and noticed that of course he was making for the biggest.

The Big Shag grabbed the bream greedily, for it wasn't often he got such a fine fish. It filled his mouth completely, and his beak was stretched to its utmost to hold it. The bream squirmed and struggled, but the Big Shag held him firmly.

As birds never swallow fish under water, the Big Shag immediately swam to the surface and flew to a post near by. The mullet and flathead were watching him with delight, for it was all happening as they had arranged, and now the youngsters understood their elders' plan. They swam along after the Big Shag, and poked their heads out of the water to watch him.

The Big Shag was in a fix. He was really very hungry, and wanted to eat the bream quickly, but though he tried with all his might, he could not get him down his throat. He gulped and squirmed, and wriggled his long neck, but not an inch farther down would that bream go.

The mullet and flathead were delighted to see their enemy in such distress, and they poked their heads out of the water and laughed, and a young flathead called out—

"Green eyes greedy!"

This made the Big Shag furious, and he made one final effort to swallow the bream, thinking that he would then go and catch the others.

But it was no use. He strained and strained, but though he stretched his beak till it nearly broke, the bream would not go down.

At last, in despair, he found that he could not eat this fine fish for his dinner, and that he must let it go. Then to his horror, he discovered that the bream would not go up. The spiky fin on its back was caught in his throat, and the bream was stuck fast. The Big Shag coughed and wriggled, but not an inch would that bream move.

Here was a fix. What was he to do? If the bream would not move, it must stay where it was; that would mean that he would never catch any more fish, and then he would starve to death. Oh, it was horrible! If only he hadn't taken the biggest bream! He wished he had been satisfied with mullet and flathead. He wished he had not quarrelled with his cousins, for then they might have pulled this horrid fish out of his mouth. It was hurting him dreadfully now, and he wondered how much longer the pain would last.

A noise behind him made him look round, and there were a lot of terns flying about and laughing at him. Then he saw that on the fence across the water were several of his cousins, and they also were laughing at him; while just beneath, in the water, the little fish were shaking with delight.

He was furious. To think that he, the Big Shag, should be a laughing-stock for all these small fry. Oh, it was too much. He must get rid of this fat bream, and then he would teach them not to laugh at him. He made one last great effort to swallow the bream—and choked. The next minute he had fallen off his post into the water; his greediness had killed him!

Nobody mourned for the greedy Shag, for he had richly deserved his punishment. And as for the bream that had choked him—well, if he had not been so vain about his swimming, the Big Shag would not have caught him; so he was punished, too.

THE WHITE HERONS

FROM AMONGST the leaves of the tall gum tree came shrill cries of joy from the mother bird, mingled with feeble baby calls. The air was full of noises and excitement, for that very morning the four pale blue eggs of the white heron had broken, and four soft fluffy heron chicks had come out. No wonder Mrs. Heron was excited; no wonder that she called proudly to her friends across the branches to tell them the joyful news, for the chicks were all as fine and strong as heron chicks could be.

The mother was so proud of them, that every few minutes she would stand on the edge of the nest, look fondly at them for a while, touch each one gently with her beak, and then, with a joyful gurgle, snuggle down upon them again. And very beautiful she looked, with pure white feathers gleaming against the dark leaves and twigs around her, and her fine white plumes floating gently in the soft breeze.

Dearly as she loved to be with her babies, she could not stay with them all day; for even the strongest and finest chicks will grow weak if they are not fed. So every now and then she would fly down from the nest to the swamp beneath, and in a few minutes return with something for the children to eat. Sometimes she carried back a frog in her long beak, sometimes a snail, sometimes a little fish, for the swamp was full of such small creatures. But whatever she brought was welcomed by the chicks, who greedily gobbled up every morsel they could get.

Day by day the little birds grew bigger and stronger, till at last they were able to raise their heads above the nest and peep out into the big world beyond. And then began such cries of excitement, and such questioning, that the mother was kept busy answering them every minute she wasn't away finding food. They wanted to know what everything round them was, and why, and when, and how; and they all spoke together, and asked so many questions in one breath, that at last the mother had to make a rule that only one chick should speak at once, and he must ask only one question at a time.

"Snappy is the biggest," said the mother, "and he shall speak first. What do you want to know, Snappy?"

"I want to know," said Snappy eagerly, "why we don't live in a tree by ourselves instead of having all those other nests near us?"

"Ah," replied his mother, "that is a very sensible question, and this is the answer. This Bush in which the tree grows is a place where many bad birds dwell. The cruel, nasty falcons, and the wicked, thieving ravens live not far away, and if they found a white heron's nest alone in a tree they would soon steal the eggs, or kill the chicks. But when they see a lot of herons near each other they are more afraid to come, for we can help each other to drive the wicked robbers away. So that is why we don't live alone in a tree, my child."

The little ones snuggled up against her and shivered fearfully as she spoke of the cruel bad birds.

"Are you sure they won't come now?" asked Snappy, as

he gazed timidly round.

"Oh, no, there is no need for fear now, my babies," said the mother, spreading her soft wings round them; "you are too big for the falcons to touch, and the ravens like eggs best. Now, Fluffy, it's your turn to ask a question."

"I want to know why we live in a swamp. This morning I heard some birds talking as they flew past, and one said: 'There are those herons in the swamp again,' and the other said: 'Yes, I wonder they don't get rheumatism in such a damp place.' Why do we live in a swamp, mother, if it's a damp place?"

The mother laughed merrily before she answered: "Why do we live in a swamp? Because, my dear, we could not live anywhere else. The swamp is full of frogs and snails and little fishes and all good things for young herons to eat, and we make our homes just above the water so that we can easily bring food to our little ones. If I had to fly a long, long way to find your meals, you would not get enough to eat, and instead of being fine strong children, you would be weak, miserable birdlets. The birds you heard talking probably don't like frogs and fish, and so they can't understand anyone living near a swamp; but it is the very best place in the world for herons to live, unless they like to be hungry."

"We don't like being hungry," laughed the little ones all together. "We like snails and frogs better than hunger," said Fluffy, and they all giggled at the joke.

"It's my turn now," cried Billy (they called him that because his bill was so long). "I want to know why we live in such a high tree. If it's good to be near a swamp, why don't we live quite close to the water, instead of away up here?"

"I'm not surprised at your asking that question," said his mother, looking at him with pride. "It's a very reasonable thing to ask. But, my dears," and she lowered her voice, and spoke very solemnly, "we have another enemy of whom I have not told you yet. He is a deadlier foe than even the falcons and ravens; his name is man. He does not fly as we do, but walks upon the ground, and so we build our homes as far up in the trees as we can, so that he will not be able to reach us, for he shows no mercy."

The little ones drew closer yet to their mother and hid their heads beneath her wings while she spoke, and the mother bent lovingly over them, but she had no words with which to soothe their alarm of this new enemy.

After a little time she tried to change their thoughts, and turning to the smallest chick said gaily: "Now, Downikins, what is your question?"

Little Downy looked admiringly at her mother before she asked her question. "I want to know why you have those beautiful white plumes, and why all the other mother herons have them, and the birds that fly past have none?"

A look of pain came into the mother's eyes as she listened; when she answered there was no more gaiety in her voice, nothing but sadness and fear.

"My dearest, those plumes which you think so beautiful are the tragedies of our lives. Without those white feathers we should be as happy and safe as any birds, for man would not take any particular notice of us. It is because he admires our plumes that he is our deadliest enemy. It is to have those plumes for his own that he comes and kills us with fire and things he calls guns. So, my children, if you do not wish to grieve me, never speak of my plumes again."

"But, mother, mother," sobbed Downy, "why does he take your beautiful plumes? Why does he want to have them?"

"He has no need of them," said the mother, "for they do not help him to live. But he gives them to his wife, and she wears them on her head and thinks she is beautiful."

"Oh, how cruel, how cruel!" wept Downy.

"I'm sure she doesn't look as lovely as you do with them, mother dear!" cried Billy.

"She's an ugly old thing," cried Snappy, "and I'd like to peck out her eyes."

"Oh, my son, you mustn't say that," said his mother gently. "Even though man is cruel to us, we must not be unkind."

"But can't we punish him for his cruelty?" asked Snappy.

"I'm sure he deserves it," cried Billy.

"Yes, he does deserve punishment," agreed the mother, "but it is not in our power to give it. Perhaps mother Nature has her own way of making him suffer for his cruelty; we can do nothing but try to avoid him."

"Oh, mother, mother!" sobbed little Downy, "I was so proud of your beautiful plumes, and now I wish you had none."

"There, there, my Chickabiddies, you must not fret or think any more about it. Put your heads under my wings and I'll tell you a story."

So the little ones crowded up to her, and she told them such a funny story about a big fish and a little fish, that they were soon laughing merrily, and forgot all about their enemy, man.

But the very next day, just after daylight, when the little ones were sleepily thinking they would like some breakfast, they suddenly felt their mother push their heads down beneath her breast, and heard her whisper: "Lie still, lie still, there is danger near."

The children shrunk down into the nest as far as they could without a word; for they knew by the tone of their mother's voice it was no time to ask questions. They could feel her breast throbbing loudly as she pressed against them, as if she were trying to hide herself within the shelter of the nest.

"Keep very still, my children," she whispered at last, "and don't make a sound. It is a man with a gun. But perhaps he won't see us," and she crouched still closer to them.

But, alas! no matter how low she huddled down upon them her tail stood out beyond the nest, and the silky white plumes gleamed in the morning sunlight.

Their brightness caught the eye of the man below; his face shone with a cruel triumph as he raised his gun towards the heron's nest.

"Bang, bang!" went the shot, raising echoes through the still bush. The mother Heron lifted her head with a quick cry of pain, stretched her wings as if to fly away from the danger, then with a helpless little flutter fell from her nest into the swamp below. Her beautiful white feathers were stained with red as she fell.

The man laid down his gun and picked her up. She was quite dead.

"She was a beauty," he said, then plucked out her lovely long plumes, threw her poor body far out into the water, and went on his way.

And up in the nest above the four little heron babies shivered with fright. They had heard the loud bang of the gun, and their mother's cry of pain. They had felt her jump from the nest, and seen her go over the edge; but they had not seen the cruel red stain on her feathers; and they had not seen the man pluck out her plumes and throw her body into the water. For in spite of their fear, they had obeyed their mother's last words to keep still, and had not moved from the bottom of the nest.

All through the morning they lay quite still; but, as every hour passed, they grew more and more terrified and lonely, and at last they felt so hungry, too, that they could no longer wait in patience. So they peeped over the edge of the nest to look for their mother, but not a sign of her could they see. They did not know that one of the many white specks on the water below was all that was left of her. They had heard the gun going bang! bang! at intervals all through the morning, and thought she was keeping away from the danger. But now the banging noise had died away in the distance, and they thought there was no longer anything to fear.

"She'll soon came now," said Billy, "for it's dinner-time, and she never forgets our dinner."

"I would like some breakfast first," said Snappy, "for I'm very hungry."

"I want some breakfast and some dinner, too," said Fluffy.

"I'm hungry too," said little Downy, "but want my mother most."

"We all want her," said Fluffy. "Let us call her and tell her the man's gone."

So they lifted their heads and all together called as loudly as they could: "Mother, mother, come back! it's safe now."

But though they cried again and again, no answer came.

So the day wore on, and when evening came the little birds were all wretchedly hungry. They saw other herons flying past with food in their beaks, and cried out to them to be fed, but the mothers were intent on feeding their own children, and had no time to find food for the little orphans whose own mother lay dead in the swamp below.

At last, tired and miserable, and very hungry, the four babies nestled closely together for warmth and fell asleep, saying to each other that perhaps their mother would come back next day.

When the morning came there was still no sign of her, and the little ones cried pitifully to the birds that passed to bring them some breakfast, for they were nearly starving. But the other mothers were just as busy as they had been the night before, and could not wait to feed them.

At last Snappy said: "I can wait no longer; I must have something to eat. I am the strongest and biggest, and I am going to fly down to the swamp to get something for myself."

"I'll come too," said Billy, valiantly.

"No, you must stay with the others and take care of them. If I can find anything, I'll bring it back."

So Snappy climbed out on the edge of the nest, and looked down at the water below. It seemed a very long way, and for a moment he felt frightened. Then his hunger mastered all other feelings, and, spreading his wings wide, as he had often seen his mother do, he jumped over the side.

The feeling of nothing under his feet filled him with terror, and he beat his wings rapidly up and down; but the little wings were not strong enough to hold him up, and quivering and fluttering he fell down, down, till with a splash he reached the swamp. Just one terrified little shriek he gave; then the water closed over him and he knew no more. In a little while he came once again to the surface, but his lifeless eyes were closed and his body floated silently on the water.

Up in the nest the other three waited and waited for their big brother's return. When the daylight was fading, and still he had not come, Billy said he would go and look for him.

"Ah, no, no, don't leave us, Billy!" sobbed the little sisters; "we are so frightened in the dark."

"But I must try to get something to eat, or we shall all die of hunger," said Billy. "I shall not be long, and perhaps I'll find Snappy." So he gently stroked their feathers, said good-bye, and then pushed himself out of the nest.

But, alas! for all his brave heart, his little wings were even weaker than his brother's; with scarcely a struggle he fell headlong into the swamp and was instantly drowned.

Left to themselves the two little sisters huddled closely together in the nest, both sobbing quietly. They were terrified at being left alone, and were too weak to look over the edge of the nest for their brothers. So they lay side by side and waited patiently. And when darkness settled down over the big bush, and the night birds called in the distance, and still their brothers had not returned, the two poor babies felt as if their hearts would break.

"Oh, mummy, mummy, why did you leave us!" sobbed Fluffy.

"It wasn't mummy's fault," wept Downy, "it was all because of that cruel wicked man. He wanted her beautiful plumes."

"Oh, I hate him, I hate him!" cried Fluffy, her anger

giving her strength for a moment. Then her voice died down, and grew weaker and weaker, as she wept piteously, "Mummy, mummy, come back!"

Her sister joined in the cry, and for a few moments the little voices wailed out on the night air; then all was silent.

And away in the city the man was proudly showing the white plumes which he had robbed from the mother's back.

THE TALE OF TIBBIE

A LARGE sea anemone once lived in a shallow pool on the rocks of the Great Barrier Reef. She was a very big and beautiful anemone, quite unlike the pretty little ones you find round Sydney. She was as big as a large cabbage, and was of the most lovely sea-green colour. There were plenty of other pretty anemones around her, hut she was the queen of them all. Her waving arms were soft like velvet, and glistened under the clear green water like fairyland flowers.

But though she was so beautiful, she was not at all vain and silly. In fact, she was just as sweet and kind as she was fair. She was very fond of all the small fishes and sea urchins who lived near her, and they all loved her. But the one she loved best was a dear little fish named Tibbie, and she was so fond of him that she let him live inside her. It may seem a funny place to live, but this anemone had such a big mouth that, when opened wide, it was almost like a room, and here little Tibbie lived very comfortably. He was a pretty little fish, about as big as a sardine, with a bright orange coat, pale yellow fins, and a nice clean white collar, of which he was extremely proud. He was a fish that anyone could have loved, and the anemone was very fond of him.

She did not even mind when he called her Annie, though her cousins teased her when they heard it, and one old anemone said:

"You shouldn't let that child be so familiar."

But Annie only laughed, and replied, "He is too little to say Anemone. And, besides, I like the name of Annie."

So Tibbie went on calling her Annie, and they were very happy together.

Sometimes he would stay out all day, playing with his friends, but he would always come back at night to his cosy little home. Annie used to worry when he stayed away all the day, for she was always afraid he might be eaten by a big fish. But Tibbie would only laugh and tell her not to worry, for he could swim as quickly as the big fish. So she did not bother him any more with her fears, but let him play and enjoy himself.

Never was there a happier little fish. All day long he would play with his little friends in the cool water. They had such fun together, playing hide-and-seek round the corals and seaweeds, or jumping up to try and catch the sunbeams as they flitted through the green water. Sometimes they would be very mischievous, and tease the sea urchins, who would try to spike them, but the little fishes were always too quick and managed to jump out of the way without being hurt. Sometimes they would be very quiet, and listen while Annie told them stories about the shark and the octopus, and the cruel big fish that ate the little fishes. The little creatures would all shiver with fright as they listened, still they enjoyed the stories very much.

The days passed by, each one very like another, and the little fishes played merrily and chased the small sea insects for their food; they lived in their pretty homes, and were just as happy as could be. Sometimes a big fish would come swimming by; then they would all rush to their homes, for most of them lived inside anemones, and, when there, they were quite safe, and could laugh at the big fish going by. But no big fish lived quite near, so as a rule they were left in peace.

One day, when they were all playing hide-and-seek round the coral, a Sea Urchin came hurrying towards them, looking very excited.

"Listen to me, listen to me!" he cried as he came near, and they all ran out of their hiding places to hear what he had to say.

"What do you think has happened?" said the Sea Urchin, mysteriously.

"We don't know," said the little fishes, all shaking their heads.

"Guess!" said the Sea Urchin.

"You have a new spike," said one.

"No!"

"You've seen the shark," said another.

"No!"

"You've killed the octopus!" said a third.

"No!"

"You're a big silly," said Tibbie.

"No!" said the Sea Urchin; and all the little fishes laughed.

"Well, what?" they asked.

"A great Red Fish has come to live in the next pool!"

"Oh!" said the little fishes in horror.

"Yes, and, what is worse, he has brought his whole family with him!"

"O-o-oh!" wailed the little fishes. "O-o-oh, how dare he! How do you know?"

"I was sleeping quietly on the rocks, when I was suddenly wakened by a great swishing in the water. It seemed to come from the next pool, so I looked over the edge, and there I saw a great big fish in a beautiful black and red coat, and with him his wife and children. There must have been about twenty of them, and I nearly fell over among them. They didn't see me, so I sat quite still and listened. I heard the big fish say:

"'This is a very nice pool, my dears. I think we'll stay here for a few weeks.'"

"Then his wife said: 'But is there anything about here to eat?' and the Red Fish replied: 'Oh, yes; there are plenty of little fishes among the anemones.' I didn't wait to hear any more, but came straight away to tell you."

When the Sea Urchin had finished speaking, the little fishes all looked sadly at each other. Then one said:

"Whatever shall we do?"

For a moment nobody answered, and then one very small fish said:

"Let us run home."

"What's the good of that?" said another. "We can't stay at home always. We must come out to get things to eat."

"Pooh!" cried Tibbie. "Who's frightened of the old fish? I'm not," and he puffed his chest out to look very big.

The other little fishes looked at him admiringly.

"Aren't you really frightened, Tibbie?" asked one.

"Of course I'm not," said Tibbie, boastingly.

"Who cares for the Red Fish? They couldn't catch me. I think I'll go and have a look at them," he added, daringly.

The other little fishes stared in amazement, and thought him very brave, but none of them would venture to go with him. So they all swam away to their homes, whilst Tibbie started off to see the new arrivals.

At the edge of the pool was a thick fringe of seaweed, and here Tibbie hid, for he did not want the Red Fish to see him. He peeped through the branches of the seaweed, and there he saw a sight which, in spite of all his courage, made him very uneasy.

There were about twenty fishes in the pool, some much larger than others, but the very smallest was at least ten times as big as Tibbie. They had great wide mouths, and large hungry eyes, and they all looked as if they could easily eat a dozen little fishes for one meal.

Tibbie was really a brave little fellow, but he felt very frightened when he saw all these hungry monsters so close to him. He thought he would not wait to speak to them, and was just turning round to go back, when he heard a squeaking voice say, quite close to him:

"Oh, Ma, do come and look at this funny little fish."

Tibbie turned round quickly, for he did not like being called a "funny little fish," and, forgetting his fear and his grammar, said angrily:

"Who are you calling names?"

The Red Fish laughed rudely, and called out: "Oh, do come and look at him. He's angry now!"

In a moment Tibbie was surrounded by the school of Red Fish. He was too angry to be afraid, or to think of running away; so he stayed where he was without thinking of his danger.

"What's the matter with you?" asked one Red Fish.

"Nothing," said Tibbie, shortly.

"Have you got toothache?" asked another.

"No!" said Tibbie.

"Then why do you have your face tied up with a white handkerchief?" asked another. At this they all burst out laughing most rudely.

For a moment Tibbie did not know what they meant, and then suddenly he realized that they were laughing at his collar—his beautiful snowy white collar, of which he was so proud! He had never been so insulted in his life before, and he shouted at them:

"You are a set of dunces if you can't tell the difference between a collar and a handkerchief, and you're a lot of rude creatures."

The Red Fishes stared in astonishment, for they had not thought so small a fish would dare to answer them back in such a way. Then the mother Red Fish said angrily:

"You impudent sprat! I'll eat you up," and she made a rush at him. But before she could reach him, Tibbie had dived under the seaweed, and was swimming as hard as he could for the other side. The Red Fish tried to follow him, but she was too big and was caught in the prickly branches.

When Tibbie had safely escaped from the Red Fish, he hurried home to tell Annie about the way he had been laughed at. He was very, very cross, and said:

"I'll punish them for laughing at me and my beautiful collar. Handkerchief, indeed! Toothache, indeed! I'll teach them the difference between a handkerchief and a collar!"

"But what can you do, dear?" said Annie. "You are too small to punish them."

"Oh, I'll do something. You wait till tomorrow," and he

went off to bed.

He stayed awake a long time thinking and thinking of some way to punish the Red Fish, though when at last he fell asleep, he had not been able to form any plan that would do.

But the next morning he forgot all about the insult to his collar, for he had something more serious to think about.

When he went out to join his little friends as usual, he found only two, and they looked too white and frightened to play.

"What's the matter?" he asked. "Where are the others?"

"Oh, haven't you heard?" said one little fish.

"No," said Tibbie. "Heard what?"

"Early this morning, when our little friends came out to get their breakfasts, the whole family of Red Fish came rushing along and ate them all up."

"Oh, the cruel, cruel monsters!" cried Tibbie.

The two little fishes were weeping bitterly, while they said:

"All our playmates are gone, and the Red Fish will come and eat us next."

"Not if I know it," cried Tibbie, valiantly; "we must do something to punish them for that."

"We're too small to do anything," wept the two little fishes. "We're going home to hide from them."

"Don't be such cowards," cried Tibbie; but the two little fishes replied:

"We're not cowards, but we don't want to be dinners," and so saying they swam away, leaving Tibbie alone.

Tibbie did not notice that they had gone, for his whole mind was filled with thoughts of how to punish the wicked

Red Fish for eating his little friends. He thought and thought, but could think of nothing that would do, and at last, in despair, he decided to go home and tell Annie all about it.

Anemone was very sad and sorry when she heard of the fate of the little fishes. She listened while Tibbie talked, and when he said angrily that he wished he was the shark, so that he could eat them up, she did not appear to hear him, for she was thinking hard. At last she said:

"How big did you say the Red Fish were, Tibbie?"

"About ten times as big as me," Tibbie answered.

"Do you think they are fast swimmers?"

"I don't think they can swim very fast, indeed, for they couldn't catch me before I got into the shelter of the seaweed." Anemone didn't speak for a while; then she said:

"Are you nervous, Tibbie?"

"No," said Tibbie, indignantly; "you know very well I'm not."

"Would you be frightened to go to the Red Fishes' pool again?"

"No!" replied Tibbie.

"Then I have a plan to punish them which I think we can carry out. But first you must bring the Red Fish here one by one."

"How can I do that?" cried Tibbie.

"You must make them chase you, and you must swim straight to me as hard as you can, and they will follow you."

"But what will you do to them when they do come here?" asked Tibbie.

"Wait and you shall see," replied Anemone. "But the first thing for you to do is to bring them here."

"I'll soon do that," cried Tibbie, starting away at once.

"Remember, you bring only one at a time," Anemone called after him.

Now, that was not so easy. If he went straight up to the Red Fishes' pool and made them chase him, they would probably all come after him together, and that would not do. He must think this out. So he rested beneath the shelter of a coral branch to consider the matter.

He hadn't been there a minute when he saw a young Red Fish swimming along towards him. He was quite alone, and was looking for his dinner.

As soon as he caught sight of Tibbie, he cried:

"Hullo, young toothache. Lend me your handkerchief."

"Booh," cried Tibbie. "You don't know a collar when you see it.

Dunce, dunce, double D,
Can't say your ABC."

"Oh, oh, you pert young sprat," said the Red Fish; "just wait a minute, and I'll have you for dinner."

He rushed towards Tibbie with his ugly mouth wide open. But Tibbie wasn't silly enough to wait for him. He darted out from the coral, calling as he went:

"Come on, dunce; come and catch me."

The Red Fish was furious, and came tearing after him as hard as he could. But Tibbie had a good start, and kept well ahead. They raced past the corals, the seaweed, the starfish, and the sea urchins. Several anemones waved their arms to Tibbie to take shelter with them, for they all thought the Red Fish would catch him.

But Tibbie kept on and on, till at last he came in sight

of his own dear Annie. She saw him coming, with the Red Fish giving chase, and waving her arms encouragingly, she called to him:

"Quickly, Tibbie; quickly."

The Read Fish heard her too, and, fearing that his prey was going to escape, he made a fresh effort, and almost caught up to Tibbie. The smaller fish heard his pursuer draw nearer, and for a moment he was afraid that he would be caught. He could see Anemone just ahead, but it seemed a long way to go with the Red Fish so close behind. If only she were a little nearer! He hoped her mouth would be wide open waiting for him. The Red Fish was almost touching his tail; in a few seconds he would be upon him.

"Annie, Annie!" he called. "Help me!"

Anemone opened her mouth wide; he made one last effort, and the next moment he was safe inside, just as the Red Fish reached him!

Then happened a strange thing. The Red Fish was swimming so hard that he could not stop himself, and he dived right into Anemone's mouth after Tibbie. Instantly, Anemone's arms closed round him, clutching him tight. In vain he struggled and squirmed. He was captured. Slowly Anemone clasped him tighter and tighter, and in a little while he was dead.

Tibbie looked on in silent awe, and when he saw that the Red Fish was killed, he asked Anemone:

"What are you going to do with him, Annie?"

"Eat him," replied Anemone. "I am very fond of fish, and they are my proper food, but I do not often get a chance to have one. The only way I can catch them is to grab them when they come chasing you."

And one by one nearly the whole of the Red Fishes chased Tibbie, and were caught and eaten by Anemone, until the remainder of the family, finding out what had happened became afraid of living so near the Anemone, and were even frightened to chase any little fishes at all. So they went away to deeper waters, and the little fishes were left in peace.

But you must not think that it was mere revenge that made the Anemone eat the Red Fish, for, unless she had big fish to eat sometimes, she could not live; nor, indeed, was it really cruelty that made the Red Fish eat the little fish, for they had also to feed on something, just as men eat sheep and cattle. And that is what wise men call "the survival of the fittest;" for it is one of the laws of Nature that the strongest shall always devour the weakest. Still, it is very hard for the little fish, isn't it? I don't wonder that Tibbie rebelled against such a law. Do you?

THE BIRDS' ALPHABET

THE AUSTRALIAN birds were having a meeting to consider what they could do to become better friends with the Humans.

All the birds of the land were gathered together, and even the birds from the sea. It wasn't very comfortable for the sea birds, as they were not used to sitting on trees, and the Albatross could not balance himself, but kept falling from side to side, till a Cocktail asked him if he should bring him a bucket of water to sit in. This made all the birds laugh so much that at last the Emu had to call for order, and then the meeting began.

"The first thing to do," said the Pelican, "is to bring ourselves into notice."

"You wouldn't have much trouble to do that," sneered the Kookaburra, at which all the little birds tittered, for the Pelican's beak is very long and big.

But they didn't laugh long, for the Pelican opened his mouth wide, and said angrily: "If you small fry don't keep quiet, I'll swallow you all."

"Order, order!" said the Emu. "We must not begin with a quarrel."

"Well, you make that old jackass keep his nonsense to himself," growled the Pelican.

"As the Pelican has already remarked," said the Emu, "the first thing to do is to bring ourselves into notice. Now how are we to do it?"

"Have our portraits taken," said the Native Companion, who knew she was handsome.

"Oh, but that wouldn't teach them our names," said the Albatross, who knew that he never looked his best in a photograph.

"Let us have a procession through the streets," said a Blue Crane, who was an elegant walker.

"Oh, yes, and get snared and put into cages," objected the Parrot, and all the other small birds agreed with him.

"No, I don't think any of those ways would do," said the Emu. "We must make them hear of us in some way."

"I know," suddenly called out a small, brown bird in a clear, sweet voice. "Let us sing songs about ourselves."

It was the Reed-Warbler who spoke, and he was noted for his good singing. Several of the birds called out, "That's a good plan. We agree to that. Let us sing songs about ourselves," and then they all shouted, "Agreed, agreed."

"Very fine," said the Kookaburra, who was in a very bad temper, "but where are you going to get the songs?"

The birds all looked at each other in dismay. They hadn't thought of that. It was easy enough to sing songs if you had them, but there were no songs written about them, although there were plenty about English skylarks and cuckoos.

"Well, we must have some written," said the Emu at last.

"Who will write them?" asked the Parrot.

That was a difficult question, and again they all looked at each other. No one had an answer ready, and it seemed as if there would be no songs written. The Kookaburra began to laugh scornfully, and said in a jeering way, "Your plan does not seem to have much chance, Mister Emu."

But suddenly a little, olive-green bird flew down into the centre of the group, and said in a sweet voice, "Please, Mister Emu, I have a suggestion to make."

"Very well, Silvereye," said the Emu, "let us have it."

The little bird drew himself up with an important air, and said, "I propose that we all make up songs about ourselves. Let us begin with the letter A, and go through the alphabet, and every bird must sing a song when it comes to his initial."

"That is an excellent plan," said the Emu. "I think we'll adopt it."

"Agreed, agreed," cried the birds, whilst the Silvereye modestly retired to the background to his friends the little Tits and Tomtits.

"How did you think of such a good idea, Sivie?" asked the little Tits.

The Silvereye looked round to see that no one was listening, and then he whispered quietly, "I knew there was no one whose name began with Z except me!"

"But yours doesn't," said a Tomtit, "Silvereye begins with S."

"Yes, but my real name is 'Zosterops,' and that begins with Z."

"Oh, what a name!" cried the little Tits. "Where did you get it?"

"The man at the Museum calls me that, so it must be right, and there are no other Z's."

"You're rather cunning, Sivie," said the little Tits.

"Silence! you youngsters," called the Emu. "We are going to begin." Then he cleared his throat, and said in a loud voice, "As A is the first letter we had better begin with that. Let me see, what does A stand for?"

"A stands for Albatross," shrieked the sea birds in chorus.

"Then let the Albatross come here into the centre of the circle and sing about himself," said the Emu.

The Albatross made an effort to get off the branch where he was sitting, but he is always a slow bird at starting, though he goes like the wind when he is flying.

Before he could reach the ground, a long-legged bird with a long turned-up bill walked into the centre.

"A is for Avocet," he said grandly.

"A is for 'Ave-a-nose, I should think," said a little Tit, and all the little birds began to giggle.

"Order!" cried the Emu, while the Avocet looked round indignantly."

"Go on, Avocet," said the Emu. "As you begin with A, and the Albatross is so slow, you must make your song."

"A is for Avocet
With a beautiful nose,"

began the long-legged bird, but he was interrupted by the Kookaburra, who called out in a loud voice—

"It's trying to get
To the sky I suppose."

He then burst out laughing, while some of the other birds laughed too, for the Avocet's nose is quite different from any other bird's in being turned up at the end.

"Order!" called the Emu, "let the Avocet finish his song." But the Avocet was too angry, and stalked proudly away.

"Well, let us go on to the next," said the Emu. "What does B stand for?"

"Blue-wren," said a small, long-tailed blue and black bird, as he hopped into the centre.

"Bower Bird," said a beautiful, sheeny-blue bird, running in front of the Emu.

"Yes, I think it must be for Bower Bird," said the Emu, and the small bird with the long tail retired with a downcast air.

The Bower Bird flew backwards and forwards as he sang—

"B is for Bower Bird,
Happy and gay.
He builds a fine bower
In which he can play."

"Very good, very good," called the birds as they applauded.

"C comes next," said the Emu. "What does C stand for?"

"Cocktail," said the little bird with the long tail, as he again hopped into the centre.

"No, C is for Cockatoo," shrieked a big, white bird with a yellow crest, as he flew down.

The small bird looked at him for a moment, then, as the big bird was more than twenty times his size, he hopped away quickly, looking very disappointed.

"Never mind," said the kind-hearted Jacky Winter to

him, "your turn will come later on."

The Cockatoo had a very loud voice, and he began his song in a shriek that nearly deafened the others—

"C is for Cockatoo
With a fine crest of yellow.
Who makes us all deaf
With his horrible bellow,"

interrupted the Kookaburra quickly.

The Cockatoo was so surprised that he just shrieked, and flew back to his place.

"I think we had better have another song for C," said the Emu, "for no one will want to sing that. Won't you make a song, Curlew?"

A tall, sad bird walked slowly into the centre, and began in a mournful voice—

"C is for Curlew
Whose voice is so sad,
It makes lonely people
With horror turn mad."

"Oh-oh, he gives me the shudders," said a Jacky Winter, "I do hate those sad songs. I wish they had let you sing your song, Cocktail, instead."

"I'm sure it would have been brighter than that," said the Cocktail.

"D," called the Emu. "Who stands for D?"

A tiny, spotted bird crept into the centre, and said in a squeaky voice, "I am a Diamond Bird; will I do?"

"You're very small," said the Emu, stooping down to look at her.

"It's time a small bird sang," called out a little Tit, "all the others have been big fellows."

"Very well," said the Emu, "you may sing." So the little bird sang in a tiny voice—

"D is for Diamond Bird
Fluffy and round,
I lay my white eggs
In a hole in the ground."

"That's a very pretty little song," said the Emu, when she had finished, and the little bird crept shyly away.

"She's silly to tell where she makes her nest," said a Tomtit. "How does she know the Cuckoo is not listening?"

"E comes next," called the Emu. "What does E stand for?"

"Emu, of course," said the Kookaburra scornfully. "Won't you make a pretty song about yourself, Mister Chairman?"

The Emu looked rather annoyed and uncomfortable, but before he could answer the Kookaburra, the Parrot shouted: "Yes, E is for Emu," and then all the birds sang in chorus—

"E is for Emu
Stately and grand,
He is the emblem
Of our native land."

When they had finished, the Emu looked very pleased as he said: "Thank you very much. You are all very kind.

Let us go on to F."

"F is for Flycatcher," said several birds together, and they all flew down to the centre and stood in a row. There were Jacky Winter, Willy Wagtail, two Miss Fantails, the Razor Grinder, and several others.

"Which of you will make the song?" asked the Emu, for several of them were good singers.

"All of us," they replied, and together they sang—

"Flycatchers all are we,
Happy as birds can be.
In an elegant way
Our tails we display
As anyone here can see."

Here they all wagged their tails from side to side, and went on to the second verse—

"Insects and flies we eat,
Thinking them nice and sweet;
We dart on the wing
And snap up each thing
That's likely to give us a treat."

The other birds here burst out in loud applause, and the Flycatchers all bowed, wagged their tails, and flew back to their places.

"That was really a very fine song," said the Emu.

"Very vain song," sneered the Kookaburra. "I should like to know why they are so proud of their tails. They are very ordinary tails."

"I think you would be proud if you had one half as good," said the Parrot, and the other birds laughed, for the Kookaburra has a very small tail for his size.

"G comes next," said the Emu, "who stands for G?"

"We do," said the Gulls and Gannets, all flying down in a flock.

"Well, which of you is going to sing?" asked the Emu.

"The Gulls," said the Gannets.

"No, the Gannets," said the Gulls.

"This won't do," reproved the Emu. "One of you must sing the song."

"The Gannet began it," called out a little Tit, which of course made all the other Tits giggle.

"Well, the Gulls must finish it if we begun it," said a Gannet.

"But we can't sing," squawked the Gulls.

"Neither can we," squawked the Gannets.

"This is awkward," said the Emu, looking worried, but before he had time to say another word the Kookaburra shouted: "As the Gulls and Gannet's can't sing a song for themselves, I'll make one for them—

"The Gannet and Gull
Are too thick in the skull
To make up a rhyme;
And so to save time
I'll sing one myself."

"Pooh!" shouted the little birds, "do you call that poetry?"

The Emu looked very grave as he said sternly to the Kookaburra, "It's not only very bad poetry, but it's very bad manners." At which the Kookaburra burst out laughing.

"We haven't yet had a song for G. Isn't there any other G?" asked the Emu.

A funny little grey bird with a sleek, round body and short legs waddled into the centre. It was the Grebe, whom some people call the Dabchick.

"I'm a G," he said.

"Very well, you sing a song," said the Emu.

The little bird stood alone in front of the chairman, and, lifting up his little head, made a very funny little noise, just like a nannygoat. He kept this up for several minutes, till even the most sedate birds were laughing, and the little birds were nearly bursting.

"He must be a G," shrieked a little Tit, "for G stands for Goat."

The little bird took no notice, but went on with his funny noise, till at last the Emu had to say: "Thank you, I think you have sung enough."

The little bird bobbed his head and waddled away.

"Still we have no song for G," said the Emu.

"I'll make one," said a little brown bird shyly. "I'm the Grass-bird," and he began to sing in a quiet voice—

"G is for Grass-bird,
Too shy to speak,
He whistles all night
In the reeds of the creek."

"Ah, that's better," said the Emu. "And now let us go on to the next, for we really must not spend so much time on one letter. Who stands for H?"

A lot of birds of different sizes and colours flew down. Some were brown, some green, some black and yellow, but they all had the same kind of long sharp beak. They stood round in a circle and began all together—

"H is for Honeyeater—"

Here they were interrupted by the Kookaburra, who gave a loud laugh and said—

"H is for Honeyeater,
Of which there are dozens,
Fathers and brothers,
And uncles and cousins."

The Honeyeaters were too angry and insulted to go on with their song, so they all flew back to their places, poking out their long feathery tongues at the Kookaburra as they passed.

"Kookaburra," said the Emu sternly, "if you cannot behave better, you will have to leave the meeting." Then, pointedly turning his back to the interrupter, he asked, "Who will sing next?"

"I," said a white bird with a long curved beak which almost reached the ground. He walked slowly up to the Emu in a very grave manner and said: "I is for Ibis. I am the Ibis.

"Oh, yes," said the Emu, "of course I know you. Will you sing a song about yourself?"

"I can't sing," said the grey bird gravely.

"Then who is to make a song about you?" asked the Emu. "Any one who likes." The Emu looked round with a puzzled air fearing that the Kookaburra would come in with something rude, but before he had a chance, a little Tit jumped up and said: "I know one about him—

"I is for Ibis
Whose nose is so long
You really can't put him
In such a small song."

The Emu was afraid that the Ibis would be offended at this, but he just turned and looked at the little Tit gravely, and, shaking his head sadly, said: "That's quite true. That will do." Then he walked wearily away.

"Now for J ," said the Emu.

Immediately all the birds shouted together—

"J is for Jackass
That silly old fowl,
Who giggles and laughs
With a horrible howl.

"He says silly things
And thinks himself clever,
But a more stupid bird
You couldn't find ever."

As they sang they all pointed at the Kookaburra, who shook with rage on his branch.

"How dare you call me a Jackass?" he shouted. "You know my name is Kookaburra."

"They call you a Jackass because you are so stupid," said

the Emu, "and I must say you have brought it on yourself. Now let us go on to K."

"K is for Kookaburra," cried the Kookaburra quickly, but all the others called out: "Oh, no, your song has been sung, and you cannot have another. K is for Kestrel."

"Yes, K is for me," said the Kestrel, looking so fierce that the Kookaburra was afraid to say another word, but sulked on his branch.

"K is for Kestrel
A fierce bird of prey,
But don't be alarmed,
He's quite gentle to-day."

sang the Kestrel, while the little birds edged away from him an a frightened manner.

"I think L comes next," said the Lyre Bird, dancing in the ring, "and of course that stands for me."

"Oh, yes, will you give us a song?" asked the Emu.

"With pleasure." And with a stately bow the Lyre Bird began to sing

"The Lyre Bird is a singer fine,
So listen to my song,
And as I haven't much to say,
It will not keep you long.

"I mimic every bird that sings,
Though he be large or small,
No bird's song is too hard for me,
But I can mimic all."

"That's very true," said the Emu, when the Lyre Bird had waltzed out of the circle. "Now for M."

"M is for Morepork," said several birds, "where is he?"

"There he is, asleep as usual," cried a little Tit. "Wake him up and make him sing."

It was hard to find the Morepork, for he was sitting on a branch of a stringy bark, and his feathers were so exactly the colour of the tree that it was hard to see which was the branch and which was the bird. But the Parrot saw him and gave him a poke with his beak, saying, "Get up and sing a song."

The Morepork stirred uneasily, and said in a grumbling voice: "Leave me alone, I want to sleep. I didn't get a wink last night."

"I am afraid your are getting into very had habits, Morepork," said the Emu gravely. "Why don't you go to bed at sunset like all well-behaved birds?" Then as the Morepork only grunted and settled himself down to go to sleep again, the Emu said: "We must have someone else for M, for we'll never waken him."

"We'll sing for you," called two birds together, as they flew down to the singing place, "we are Martins." They were both grey-blue birds and very much alike, but one had a black face and the other had white eyebrows. They were such pretty, graceful birds that it didn't seem to matter that their voices were not very pleasant as they sang—

"M is for Martin;
 Cousins are we,
And each of us builds
In the fork of a tree.

"We travel together,
And build near each other,
For we are as friendly
As brother and brother."

"Now that is the kind of song I like to hear," said the Emu, as the two Martins flew away. "Let us see if we cannot have more in the same strain. Who stands for N?"

"I do," said the Native Companion, as she walked gracefully into the centre. She was a beautiful bird with lovely, grey feathers and a long graceful neck, and as the other birds looked at her they wondered that no Australian poet had sung about her. Before saying anything she spread out her wings and danced a few steps of the minuet, then began to recite—

"N is for Native Companion so tall,
Wherever I dance
I'm the belle of the ball,
On the far western plains of the country I live,
By my beauty and grace much pleasure I give."

As she spoke she danced backwards and forwards in so pretty a fashion that none of the other birds noticed the vanity of her words except the Kookaburra. He had been silent and sulky since they had all made fun of him, but now he burst out with a loud laugh.

"Is that the tone of song you like, Mister Emu? So modest and simple. Let me add another verse," and before anyone could stop him, he shouted—

"N is for Native Companion so vain,
A long-legged lanky, decidedly plain."

"Shame, shame!" cried the birds in chorus while the poor Native Companion looked miserable, for she was not really vain, but only pleased that she could dance gracefully.

"Take no notice of him," said the Emu scornfully, "let us go on to O. Where is O?"

"Here," said a long-legged bird with a long beak. Without wasting time, he began to say in a quick voice—

"O is for Oyster-catcher
(What a horrible name!)
The crabs and fish avoid me,
But I catch them just the same."

"Very good!" shouted the sea birds, "that's an interesting song."

"Yes, it's very nice," said the Emu politely, though really he wasn't much interested in crabs and fish. "Now who stands for P?"

A queer-looking black and white bird waddled into the centre. He had feet like a duck, and instead of wings he had two funny little skinny flappers. As soon as he appeared the Kookaburra burst out laughing, and called out—

"P is for Penguin,
A funny old chap;
His two little wings
Can do nothing but flap."

Then to everyone's surprise, the Penguin turned towards the Kookaburra and said: "Thank you very much. That's just what I would have said myself, only I couldn't have put it so nicely." Then he waddled gravely away.

The Kookaburra was too astonished to reply, for he certainly had not meant to be nice, and he felt very silly at the Penguin's words.

"Q comes next. What does Q stand for?"

"Quail," called a little brown bird, as he came running up, and he sang in a sad voice—

"Q is for quail,
Whose home's on the ground;
He runs through the grass,
And makes not a sound.

"But when sportsmen come
With dog and with gun,
The poor little Quail
Finds it's no good to run."

"Poor little chap," said the Emu kindly, "You do have a bad time indeed. Now what does R stand for?"

"I'll sing for R," said a dark-blue bird about the size of a fowl. He had a bright red beak and long, red legs, and as he walked into the centre he pointed his toes and whisked up his tail to show the white feathers beneath it. He was such a handsome bird, that if he did seem rather conceited there was some excuse for him. He had a queer voice, but he began to sing—

"R is for Red-bill,
My home is so damp,
I expect you all wonder
I don't get the cramp.

"But water and mud
Are the best things for me.
And I should feel awkward
Perched up in a tree."

Then he flicked up his tail and stalked away.

"Who will sing a song for S?" asked the Emu.

An odd little bird with a little body on very long legs walked up.

"I'm a Stilt," he said, "I'll sing for S." And he sang—

"S is for Stilt,
Who lives in the reeds,
His long legs are useful
To wade through the weeds."

"T's next," cried the Emu. "Who stands for T?"

"I do. I do. I do. I do," called the Tom-tits, Tree-creepers, Thrushes, and Thickheads all together.

"Dear me!" said the Emu, "do you all begin with T? But you can't all sing, you know. Which of you will make a song?"

"None of them," cried a harsh voice. "The land birds have sung too much. I'm a Tern, and I'm going to sing now, for it's time the sea birds had a turn."

"But they always have a Tern," cried a little Tit, who

hadn't a chance to show his wit for some time.

"I think you're trying to make a joke," said the Tern, "but at any rate I'm going to have a turn now," and he sang in a wild, harsh voice—

"T is for Tern
Who skims o'er the sea,
And gracefully dives
In the waves for his tea."

"That's very nice," said the Albatross, "but it makes me feel hungry."

"Yes, it must be nearly time for tea," agreed the Emu. "We must hurry through the rest. Who is for U?"

There was no answer. The birds looked at each other in silence, and thought of each other's names, but no one knew of a U.

"Ha, ha, ha!" suddenly laughed the Kookaburra, "I'm the only U amongst you."

"But you're K," said the Emu.

"No, J," called the little Tits.

"No, I'm U," shrieked the Kookaburra. "U stands for useful, and I'm the only useful one among you, for I kill snakes!"

"Well, if no one's name begins with U, let us go on to V. Who stands for V?"

Again there was silence, and again all the birds looked at each other. The Emu was just going to say, "Go on to W," when a small bird hopped shyly up. It was a cousin to the Blue-wren, and very much like him, but it had brown patches on its shoulders, and it was much shyer than the

Bluewren. It spoke in a whisper, as if frightened of being heard, and said: "In some books I'm called the Variegated Wren. Will that do for V?"

"What a name!" said a little Tit; "no wonder he whispers it."

"Yes, that will do for V," said the Emu. "Can you sing a song about yourself?"

"V is for Variegated," began the little bird, then looked round in a frightened way, and saying, "I can't find a rhyme for that," hopped quickly away.

"It is a difficult word," said the Emu. "We won't try to find a rhyme. Let us go on to W."

"W is for Wonga," cried a big blue Pigeon, who began to sing in a plaintive voice—

"W's for Wonga
Who's so good to eat
That sportsmen will chase him
Into his retreat."

"Now for the next letter," cried the Emu. "X comes next. But who stands for X?"

"The Jackass," called a little Tit, "because he's extra silly."

"I'm afraid we'll have to leave X," said the Emu, "and go on to Y."

"I'm the only Y," said the Yellowbob. "I know I'm really a Robin, but as the Robins didn't sing, don't you think I may sing for Y?"

"Yes, I think so," said the Emu, and the Yellowbob began to sing

"Y is for Yellowbob,
Friendly am I,
I do not fear men,
And so I'm not shy."

"That's a dear little song," said the Emu. And now there's only one letter left. What does Z stand for?"

"Me!" shrieked the Silvereye, so excitedly that he could hardly get it out.

"You?" said the Emu in surprise. "Oh, I think you've made a mistake. Silvereye begins with S."

"Yes, but my proper name is Zosterops," cried the Silvereye, proudly.

"Zoster-what?" exclaimed the Emu. "Whoever told you that?"

"The man at the Museum calls me Zosterops," said the Silvereye grandly.

"Well, he ought to know," said the Emu. "Can you sing a song about it?"

"Z is for Zosterops,"

began the Silvereye, then stopped to think.

"Z is for Zosterops," he began again, and again stopped. Then before he could make a third attempt the Kookaburra called out

"Z is for Zosterops,
Oh, what a name!
No wonder the Silvereye
Stutters with shame."

At this all the little birds giggled, for they thought it great fun that the Silvereye could not make a song about himself, when he had been the one to suggest it.

"Never mind, Silvereye," said the Emu kindly, "perhaps you'll be able to finish it another time. And now, as we have gone through the alphabet, I think we should sing a chorus to conclude."

Then they all sang and their united song was so beautiful that Humans stopped in their work to listen, and admire. So the birds got the attention that they wanted, and ever since they and the Humans have been the best of friends.

THE FLOWER FAIRIES

It was a hot sunny day in October. Early in the morning Dickie's sisters had sent him out into the bush to get flowers to decorate the house; but, though he had been out a long while, and walked a long way, he had only gathered a few. For he had spent his time looking for flannel flowers, and they were very scarce.

The few flowers he had in his hand looked as flowers generally do when they have been picked by little boys. Some of them had scarcely any stalk at all, and most of them had been pulled up by the roots; so altogether it was not a very pretty bunch.

Dickie could see this for himself, and he also knew that his sisters would be very disappointed if he did not take home anything better.

"Someone must have pulled all the flannel flowers," he grumbled to himself as he walked along. This was quite true, but he did not stop to think that it was because other people had pulled the flowers up by the roots, just as he himself had done, that there were no flannel flowers left. So he went on looking all round and searching under ferns and shrubs for the flowers he wanted.

After a time he came to a little gully, where beneath the tall gums, clumps of white flannel flowers waved amongst the grey rocks.

"Oh, what beauties!" Dickie exclaimed as he saw them, and he at once began to pick them as fast as he could, tearing them up roots and all in his hurry. At last he had gathered every single one of the pretty flowers, and then he sat down to arrange them in his bunch.

It was cool and quiet in the shade, and he was very tired, so he thought he would just lie down on the ferns for a while before he set out for home. He lay flat on his back, gazing up at the blue sky through the trees. The gently waving boughs of the wattles and the gum-trees above his head made him feel drowsy, and he was just dozing off to sleep when suddenly he was aroused by the sound of someone crying very softly.

He sat up quickly and looked round. There, sitting beside his bunch of flowers was the daintiest, prettiest little fairy a boy had ever seen. She wore a white frock edged with green, and on her yellow hair was a little green cap. In her hands she held some of the flannel flowers from Dickie's bunch, and she was weeping bitterly.

Dickie sat and stared at her. He had often read about fairies, but had never seen a real live one before. He had always thought they were happy joyful beings, and was surprised to see this one crying like an ordinary little girl.

The fairy did not see him, but kept on weeping and weeping, and every now and then she kissed the flowers, and said softly "Poor things, poor things!"

Now, Dickie was really a nice little boy, and he did not like to see girls crying, so at last he said, "What's the matter, little fairy? Don't cry."

The fairy looked up quickly, and Dickie said again—

"Who are you? What's the matter. What are you crying for?"

"I am the fairy of the flannel flowers, and I am grieving for these poor flowers," said the fairy sadly.

"Why, what's wrong with them?" asked Dickie in surprise. "They're beauties."

"Yes, they were very beautiful, but now they're all dead. Some cruel being has pulled them out by the roots, and killed them."

At this Dickie looked a little bit ashamed, though he did think it silly to make so much fuss over a few flowers. The fairy saw the look, and said in a sharp voice, "Was it you who picked them?"

"Yes," said Dickie. Then as the fairy looked very angry, he added quickly: "they are for my sister to decorate with. I must take them home now."

"No," answered the fairy. "You must come with me."

"I cant," said Dickie, "I must go home."

"You must come with me," repeated the fairy.

"I won't!" cried Dickie, and he snatched up his flowers and began to run.

"Stop him," cried the fairy in a loud voice, and in an instant Dickie felt his feet caught fast by the bracken. He fell flat on his face, while the ferns put out dozens of arms and held him so fast, that he could not move.

"Now carry him to the Queen," said the fairy, and as soon as she spoke, the wattle tree above him stretched down a long arm, and picked him up into the air. For a second the wattle held him, then tossed him across to the next tree; then he was tossed to the next and the next, till he was quite out of breath. At last a tree fern caught him and held him tight. Then, very gently, so as not to hurt the young fronds, the tree fern rolled him down into the heart of his leaves. It seemed to Dick that, as he rolled, he grew smaller and smaller, until at last, when he reached the bottom, he was only as big as the fairy.

It was just as well he had grown small, for if he had stayed big there would have been no room for him, because the heart of the tree fern was crowded with fairies. As Dick rolled in, they all looked at him, and he heard a voice say, "Here he is."

It was the fairy of the flannel flowers who had spoken. She was seated on a curled-up fernfrond, beside another larger fairy who was dressed in deep red with a crown on her head, which looked to Dick like a waratah. All round her were seated other fairies in different coloured dresses. Some wore frilly gowns of white velvet, and others were dressed in yellow satin, while some wore soft pink silk, or blue gauze, and many other kinds of dresses. It seemed to Dickie that he knew them by sight, as indeed he did really, for they were the fairies of all the bush flowers, buttercups in yellow satin, boronia in pink silk, and many others that Dickie had often picked in the bush.

They sat round on the fronds of the tree fern, and as the Flannel Flower fairy spoke they all looked very hard at Dickie.

They were so small that Dick did not feel frightened of them at first, but suddenly he remembered that he also was very small now, and then he began to look round to see if he could get out. But every leaf of the tree fern was guarded by a fairy, and there was no way of getting past. So he just stayed where he was and waited.

"This is the boy who killed my flowers," said the Flannel Flower fairy to the Queen.

The Queen bent down and looked at Dick, then asked sternly—

"Why did you kill the flannel flowers?"

"I didn't kill them," said Dickie.

"O-o-oh!" said all the flower fairies together, and the white-robed fairy said, "Why, see, he still has them in his hand."

Dickie looked down, and there was his bunch of flowers still in his hand.

"I picked them for my sisters," he said, "but I did not mean to kill them."

"Then why did you pull them up by the roots?" asked the Queen.

"I did not know it would kill them," said Dickie, beginning to cry, for all the fairies looked so stern and sad, that he felt quite miserable.

"I wanted a nice bunch, and I picked them quickly, and their roots came up, but I didn't know flowers could fe-e-el," and here he began to cry just as badly as the Flannel Flower fairy had cried.

"Little boys that don't know must be taught," said the Queen. "You must learn that flowers do feel. We live to make human beings happy, and are pleased when they pick our blossoms to keep in water and brighten their rooms. But every time you pull a flower out by the roots, that flower dies, and all its children die, and no more grow from it. And if everyone pulled up the roots there would soon be no flowers left, and the world would be a very dreary place to live in."

"I do not think," the Queen went on, "that you are a wicked boy; you are just thoughtless. But you must be taught to think of other people's feelings. Now you will learn what a flower feels like when it is pulled out by the roots."

Then she turned to the fairies, and said "Teach him his lesson."

Instantly a spiky Wattle fairy flew towards him and tweaked a hair out of his head.

It hurt very much, and Dick cried out, "Stop it!" but before he could move another fairy came, and then another, and another, and each one tweaked a hair out of his head, and each hair hurt worse than the last, till he could stand no more, and he called out to the Queen, "Oh, make them stop. Please make them stop. I'll never pull another flower up by the roots. Do make them stop."

"That will do," said the Queen, "I think he has learned his lesson," and all the fairies flew back to their places.

Then the Queen turned to Dick and said kindly, "I think you will always remember now to be kind to all living things, even if they are only flowers."

"Yes, I will," promised Dickie, and he meant it.

"Now take him back," said the Queen, and the tree fern took hold of him, and began to roll him up again.

"Good-bye," he called, as he neared the top, and all the flower fairies answered, "Good-bye, good-bye," and just as he reached the edge, the Flannel Flower fairy flew after him, and pushed a big bunch of beautiful white blossoms into his hand.

"Take these," she whispered, "they will help you to remember."

He took the flowers, and the next moment was being tossed back by the tree branches, until he reached the wattle which had first lifted him up.

In a minute he was lying amongst the ferns again, with no sign of a fairy anywhere. But there was the bunch of flannel flowers to remind him of his promise to the Queen, so he knew it could not have been just a dream.

THE LION AND THE KANGAROO

ONCE UPON a time the British Lion thought he would go a-travelling. He was tired of sitting at home in his little Island, where everyone treated him with so much respect and dignity that no other animals dared to go near him; and he longed for a playmate.

"I think I'll go and see my cousin, the Kangaroo," he said to himself. "I know he will be glad to see me, and it will be fun going to a new country."

So he jumped into his boat and sailed away across the sea. He was many days on his journey, for the Kangaroo lived at the other end of the world. He did not see many other animals as he travelled, for they were all so afraid of the lion that they kept out of his way as much as possible, and so without adventures he at last reached the land of the Kangaroo.

It was a bright sunny day as he sailed through the big head-lands that guard the entrance to the Kangaroo's land, and the Lion thought he had never seen so beautiful a place.

"I did not know my cousin had such a nice country," he said to himself. "I think I shall stay for a long time."

It was so warm and sunny that he thought it was very much nicer than his own Island, where it often rains. He was a nice, kind old Lion, and though he looked fierce sometimes, he would never hurt anyone unless that person hurt him first. But now, as he basked in the sunshine, he looked as good-tempered as a Lion could be.

He had not seen the Kangaroo for many years, although they were cousins, and the last time they met was when the Kangaroo was only a child, and had gone to see the Lion in his Island, to ask him to be friends. Most of the animals wanted to be friends with the Lion, because he was the strongest of all; but the Kangaroo was the one he loved best, for as I have told you, they were cousins.

As his boat sailed up the beautiful harbour the Lion was quite excited at the thought of seeing his cousin.

"The Kangaroo will be surprised to see me," he said, "and I know he will be very pleased."

And so he sailed on till he came to the shore, and there he ran his boat up on the sand. He was just going to jump out, when he saw the Kangaroo hopping across the beach towards him.

"Hullo, cousin!" he shouted, and waved his paw.

The Kangaroo did not answer, but came towards him looking as if he were wondering whoever this new-comer could be.

"Don't you know me?" called the Lion, as the Kangaroo came nearer. "Don't you recognize your cousin?" and so saying he jumped out of the boat, and sprang to meet him.

"I have no cousins," said the Kangaroo haughtily, "and I should like to know why you come and land in my country without asking permission. Who are you?"

The Lion looker rather astonished at the Kangaroo's words, and he answered—

"I am the British Lion, and your kinsman. Surely you

haven't forgotten me. Don't you remember when you were a child you came to see me in my Island, and asked me to be friends?"

"Oh, yes," said the Kangaroo coolly, "I believe I do remember you. But as for being cousins, I don't see much in that, when you live at one end of the world and I at the other."

"But it is only because you are my cousin that I help you," replied the Lion, who was beginning to be annoyed at the way the Kangaroo was talking.

"Help me!" repeated the Kangaroo scornfully. "When did you help me? Why, I haven't even seen you for years."

"No, but the other animals know that I am your friend and cousin, and so they do not dare to attack you or try to steal your country."

The Kangaroo laughed mockingly, and said: "I am quite strong enough to protect my own land without your help."

"You did not think so when you came to ask me to be friends," replied the Lion angrily.

"Oh, that was because I was a child then, and knew no better, and I thought you were strong and powerful. But now I know that you are old, and not as strong as I am myself. I don't need your help now, and you are not strong enough to give it, if I did. So you can go and mind your own business, and leave me to manage mine," and here the Kangaroo turned his back on the Lion and walked away.

The Lion was thunderstruck, and for a moment could not speak. Then he called out after the Kangaroo—

"Ungrateful one! You'll be sorry for this."

But the Kangaroo just burst out laughing, and hopped away. So the Lion went back to his boat.

He felt very angry and hurt at the Kangaroo's behaviour, and at first he thought he would go away at once; so he said wrathfully:

"It will serve him right if I tell the Bear and the Eagle and the Dragon that he is no relation of mine, and that I won't protect him any longer. They'll soon steal his country from him," and, so saying, he jumped into his boat and began to sail away.

But as he went across the blue water and looked round on the green hills sloping down to the shore, he felt sad at the thought of this lovely land being stolen by the other animals.

"After all," he thought, "the Kangaroo is my cousin, whatever he may say. And it's only because he is so young and foolish that he is conceited enough to think he is as strong as I am. The silly fellow! It would be unkind to take notice of his vanity and rudeness, and leave him quite unprotected."

Now the Lion was old and wise, and very strong, and when people or animals are old and wise, they always make allowance for hot-headed youth. He knew that the Kangaroo was very proud of owning such a lovely land, and he knew that because the Kangaroo had just grown up, he thought he was the finest and strongest fellow in the world. But he also knew that the Bear, or the Eagle, or the Dragon, could easily kill the Kangaroo and steal his country if they liked. And he knew that if he, the Lion, had not promised to befriend his cousin, they would have done so long ago. For it was only fear of the Lion that had kept the other animals from attacking the Kangaroo's land. Many of them had gazed at it longingly, but they were all too much afraid of the lion to touch it.

Now the Lion knew this very well, and as he was really fond of his cousin, his anger soon melted and he turned his boat round and sailed back to the shore.

There he landed and began to walk across the beach to the trees on the hill-side; but he had only gone a few steps when the Kangaroo came hopping towards him.

"What, still here, you old slow-coach?" he shouted to the Lion. "I thought I told you to go away."

"I did go," replied the Lion quietly, "but because I was sorry for you, and knew you would come to harm if unprotected, I came back. For I do not wish to be unfriendly."

"It's all nonsense to talk like that," cried the Kangaroo. "You know very well that you don't come here to be friends with me. You only come because you think you can grab a bit of my country."

At this the Lion felt very angry indeed, and he said with dignity:

"You think too much of yourself, young fellow. If I wanted your country, there would be no need for me to stoop to cunning; for I could kill you with a blow of my paw, if I liked, and take the whole of your land for myself. You don't deserve the consideration and help I give you, you vain young creature, but because you are my kinsman, I will not punish you as you deserve. I shall stay here for a time, and give you a chance to learn better manners."

The Lion spoke so quietly and yet so sternly that the Kangaroo looked a bit ashamed, and he answered in a sulky tone

"Oh, well, as you are my cousin, I suppose you must stay for a while."

It certainly wasn't a very gracious invitation, but as the Lion wanted to be friends with his cousin, he accepted it, and stayed.

As the days passed, and they knew each other better, the Lion grew rather fond of the Kangaroo, for he found that, though his manners were rough, he was very good at heart, and he tried to teach him a few things about guarding his country, and how to make himself strong enough to fight the savage animals if they attacked him.

But the Kangaroo was very suspicious, and though he listened when the Lion talked, he always thought he had come only to get what he could out of his country, and that made him very rude to the Lion at times. Still, the Lion was determined not to quarrel, so when the Kangaroo was more rude and sulky than usual, he would take no notice, but wait until he was in a better temper.

Now all this time, while the Lion was staying with the Kangaroo, the other animals were wondering what had become of him. They knew he had left his Island on a journey, but did not know where he had gone. As the days passed, and they did not see a sign of him, nor hear his roar, they decided he must be dead. There was great rejoicing amongst them, and they all began to quarrel and fight (which was the thing they liked doing best), for the Lion, when on his Island, always kept an eye on them, and made them behave themselves; thus they were very glad indeed that he was not there to keep them in order, and they quarrelled to their heart's content.

The Bear and the Eagle and the Dragon, who were always jealous of the Lion's lands, began to look round to see what they could take for themselves, and the Dragon said to the other two—

"I am going down to kill the Kangaroo and take his land. Now that the Lion is dead, there will be no one to punish me, and I can easily kill that stupid young Kangaroo.

"All right," said the Bear; "you go, and I'll take care of your country while you are away."

Now, the Bear really meant to steal the Dragon's country as soon as his back was turned, but the Dragon didn't know that. So he got into his boat, and sailed away to the land of the Kangaroo.

The Lion and the Kangaroo were walking amongst the trees near the beach, and the Kangaroo was not in a very good temper. He said to the Lion:

"I don't see why you want to stay here with me, if you are not trying to steal my country. I don't want you, and I can easily protect myself and my belongings. I don't believe you like me as much as you say you do, and I think that if you got a chance you would join any foes that attacked me, or else run away and leave me to fight them alone."

"You are unjust, Kangaroo," said the Lion. "But you will learn some day that the Lion never runs away from an enemy, nor deserts a friend."

"It's all very well to talk," grumbled the Kangaroo, "but you can't prove your words."

The words were hardly out of his mouth when they were both startled by a tremendous roar. Quickly they ran towards the beach, and looked through the tea-tree bushes out to sea. There they saw a sight which made the Kangaroo's blood grow cold with horror, and made every hair on the Lion bristle with rage.

There, sailing up the bay in a flat, square boat, with a

yellow sail, was the most awful object the Kangaroo had even seen. It was a strange, hideous beast with four very ugly legs, and huge blazing eyes, while out of its mouth came great blasts of flame and smoke.

"What is it?" gasped the Kangaroo, in a frightened whisper.

"The Dragon," growled the Lion.

"What does he want? Why does he come here?"

"He wants to steal your country," replied the Lion.

At this the Kangaroo began to tremble. He had talked very bravely before about fighting any enemies, but that was because there had never been any to fight, and he had never seen any of the other animals. But now, when he saw this horrible, fearful creature coming towards him, he was terrified, and turning to the Lion, said, just like a little child

"Oh, you won't let him kill me, will you?"

"No, no," said the Lion kindly. "I will take care of you."

While they were talking, the Dragon came sailing-on towards the beach. As they were hidden behind the trees, he did not see them, but thinking there was no one about, he said to himself—

"I shall be able to land quite easily, and hide behind a tree, and when the Kangaroo comes down to bathe, I shall spring out and kill him;" then he laughed aloud and blew a great flame from his mouth.

He sailed right up to the shore, smiling hideously the while, and jumped out on to the sand. He pulled his boat up on the beach, and then walked stealthily towards the thick bushes where he meant to hide until the Kangaroo came. He was feeling very satisfied, thinking how nice it would be to possess the Kangaroo's country, which was much more beautiful than his own, when suddenly he heard an angry roar. The smile vanished from his face, and his ugly eyes grew bigger than ever with fright, as he murmured to himself in a terrified voice:

"The Lion!"

He turned quickly, and there, bounding towards him, was the Lion, with the Kangaroo at his heels. With a loud shriek the Dragon rushed towards his boat, but before he could push it into the water, the Lion was upon him.

Then began such a fight as the Kangaroo had never dreamed of. The Dragon was furious and strong with anger, and he fought valiantly. At first it seemed as if he would overcome the Lion, although the latter was so much stronger; for it was years since the Lion had fought, as all the animals were afraid to attack him, and he was rather stiff and much out of practice; whereas the Dragon was always fighting with someone, and was very active. Still the Lion's strength matched the Dragon's quickness, and so the fight was equal. Together they rolled over and over, tearing and biting, sometimes one on top, sometimes the other.

The Kangaroo stood watching them with a strange feeling in his heart. Only that day he had wished he could get rid of the Lion, and had insulted him—trying to drive him away. But now, as he gazed at the fight, he was filled with a fear that the Lion might be beaten. At first it was just alarm lest the Dragon should conquer the Lion, and then slay him, but as he looked at the old Lion fighting so bravely and fiercely, he forgot about himself, forgot the danger to his own land, and, suddenly, as he saw the Lion go down under the Dragon, his heart seemed bursting with a new affection, and he knew that he loved the Lion.

Instantly he was filled with rage against the Dragon, who thus dared to oppose his kinsman, and forgetting all his fear, he rushed madly up to the fighters.

The Lion was on his back on the sand with the Dragon crouching above him. He was really in no danger, but was taking a breath before making a final spring, and would overcome his foe; but the Dragon thought he was tired out, and his eyes blazed with the light of victory. He laughed with his hideous grating voice, and blew a blaze from his mouth, as he shouted—

"Ah, ha! Mister Lion, who's master now?"

But before he could utter another word, a great weight was hurled upon his back, and as he half turned to shake it off, long claws were dug into his side. With a shriek of pain and rage, he let go the Lion, and jumped up to face this new enemy. It was the Kangaroo!

The Dragon was astounded. He had quite overlooked the courage of the Kangaroo. And to think that this youngster should dare to attack him, one of the oldest of all the animals, was too much to put up with. Such impudence! he thought, and with a savage yell he leaped at the Kangaroo.

But the Kangaroo was too quick, and with a great hop, passed the Dragon and reached the side of the Lion. Side by side the cousins stood, and awaited the attack of the Dragon. With fresh fury he came rushing towards them, but the cousins stood shoulder to shoulder, and before he knew where he was, the Dragon was rolling on the ground. Again and again he attacked, each time only to be overturned, till at last he knew he was beaten.

Breathless and panting he lay on the sand waiting for the Lion to finish him. But the Lion was as merciful as he was strong, and instead of killing the Dragon, as he could so easily have done, he went and stood beside him saying

"You may get into your boat, and go away as soon as you can breathe. I think you have learned a lesson, friend Dragon. In future you will know better than to come to my kinsman's country."

"I didn't know you were here," gasped the Dragon.

"No, I know you didn't. And you thought that because the Kangaroo was young you could easily steal his land. But understand this: "While there is a breath of life in me, the animal that attempts to fight the Kangaroo will have to fight me also. He is my nearest and dearest kinsman, and as long as we both live, we will fight together against the world. And you may tell that to the Bear and the Eagle, and the other animals, too. Now go!"

Without a word the Dragon slowly crawled across the beach, entered his boat, and sailed away down the harbour. Just as he was getting out of sight, he shouted—

"Kangaroo, you're a lucky fellow to have the Lion for your friend." The Kangaroo heard this, and, turning towards the Lion, said—

"I have been rude and unfair to you. But I was stupid, and vain, and thought you wanted to steal my country, and I imagined I was strong enough to do without you. Now I know that I do not wish to live without your friendship and help, for I love you and need you. Can you forgive me?"

The old Lion patted him on the back, and answered—

"That's all right, my boy. You have a good heart, and though you were rather silly and vain, I knew it was only because you were so young. and I loved you in spite of yourself. We must be friends, for without me the Dragon would have killed you; and yet alone I could not have overcome him. So you see how necessary we are to each other. I am old and wise, but you are young and active, and together we can defy the world."

"Then let us stand together always, as kinsmen should," said the Kangaroo.

And they have done so ever since. And the other animals think a long time before they attack the Lion, because they know they will have to fight the Kangaroo as well. And the Kangaroo's land is safe from invaders, for they know right well that if they harm the Kangaroo they will have to answer to the Lion.

THE THREE HEROES

It was midnight in Sydney Botanic Gardens. A gentle wind crept through the trees, sighing softly as it went. The moon, just lately risen, gleamed on the leaves as they swayed in the wind, and made them glitter like stars in the frosty air. On the branches of the trees the birds were sleeping, huddled close together for warmth, and on the banks near the ponds the Black Swans with their family of Cygnets were also slumbering.

Everything was so quiet that it seemed as if the whole world was asleep. Suddenly, out of the distance, there came the cry of a Curlew, sad and wailing. Some of the little birds stirred on their branches at the sound, and the young Cygnets cuddled closer to their mother. Then, as the Curlew's note died away in the distance, a sad sigh sounded near the pond, and the Willow waved her long bare arms and, with a shudder, lifted her head and said—"Another year!"

At these words an Oak, which stood near by, lifted his head also and echoed the words, "Yes, another year." But his voice was not mournful like the Willow's, but proud and jubilant, and he shouted so loudly that the Cygnets, roused from their slumbers, sat up and stared, for they had never before heard the trees talking.

"What is it?" they asked their mother in frightened whispers. "Why are the trees talking tonight?"

"Hush!" said the mother, "do not let them hear you. This is the great night in the year for the Oak, and the saddest of all for the Willow. For the Oak loves to remember, but the Willow longs to forget."

"Remember what? Forget what?" asked the Cygnets.

"Be still and listen, and you will hear," said the mother.

Even as she spoke there came another sigh from the Willow, longer and sadder than the first, and then, waving her arms, she began to speak.

"Listen to me, all you young trees, while I tell you my sad story. I did not always live near this pond. I was born in an island far across the seas. It was only a little rocky island, but it was the saddest in the world, for there the greatest soldier that ever lived, died and was buried."

"He was not the greatest soldier," interrupted the Oak.

"I will tell my story in my own way," said the Willow, "and when I have finished you may tell yours. He was the greatest and bravest and the cleverest of soldiers, and his name was Napoleon Bonaparte."

Here the Willow sighed deeply, and the sigh was echoed by some of the other trees, but the Oak only looked stern and angry.

"On that little rocky island," went on the Willow, "that great soldier spent his last days, and there he died. My sisters and I grew beside his tomb. Very proud we were to shelter the last resting place of our hero, and gladly would I have ended my days in that sacred spot. But cruel hands cut me from my parent tree, and carried me across the sea to this strange land, and here I have lived for many, many years.

No longer can I shed sad tears above my hero's grave, but I must spend my life in this new land, where they know nothing of world-famed soldiers."

She broke off and sighed, and waved her arms in sorrow. Then in a more angry tone, she went on.

"If only I could be allowed to forget, I would not grumble. I should try to be satisfied in this new land, and pretend I had never known a glorious warrior. But each year on this hateful night of the eighteenth of June, I am forced to wake from my sleep, and remember all that happened to my hero before he was sent to my native land. Oh, oh, oh," she wailed, "I cannot, I will not tell that horrible story."

"Then I will," said the Oak in a stern voice. "It is not a horrible story, for it was on this night, many years ago, that my countryman, the Iron Duke, conquered your hero, as you call him, and saved the world from his clutches. A poor hero he was! He was greedy and cruel, and little he cared for the sorrow he caused if only he could get what he wanted. A hero should be kind as well as brave, and your Napoleon was cruel. My Iron Duke was the real hero. He conquered your Napoleon, and he was the greatest soldier in the world."

"That's not true," sobbed the Willow; "Napoleon was the greatest soldier."

"Wellington was the greatest," shouted the Oak angrily, "and all Englishmen know it."

"What does it matter now, whether either was the greatest?" said a quiet voice. "It all happened so very long ago."

The Willow lifted her head, and the Oak turned his gaze at the speaker. The little Cygnets also turned with frightened curiosity, and saw coming slowly across the lawns towards them a giant Norfolk Island Pine. Although he was very, very tall and stiff, he moved quite gracefully and easily, and was soon close beside the others.

The Cygnets stared in amazement. They crept closer to their mother, who calmed them, saying gently—"Don't be afraid. It is the old Wishing Tree. I don't know how he came here, but listen and you will probably learn."

So the Cygnets put their heads beneath their mother's wing, and lay quite still, and listened.

"Who are you?" asked the Oak, proudly, when he had recovered from his astonishment. "Who are you, and why do you interfere with us?"

"I am the Norfolk Island Pine," said the tall tree, "and I interfere because I am tired of having my rest disturbed by you two wranglers. For years this has been going on, and, as you never come to any agreement, it seems likely to go on for many more years."

"I should think we couldn't agree," wailed the Willow. "While that horrid Oak gloats over his Duke's victory and my Napoleon's defeat, we are not likely to agree."

"I don't know how you can be bothered keeping it up," said the Pine. "When you first came here I could understand, for you were both young and foolish, and it was not so long since your heroes had died. But now you are both old enough to know better, and your heroes are as dead as last year's leaves, and no one cares which was the greater."

"No one cares?" echoed the Oak. "Why, the whole Fate of Europe depends upon it."

"The whole fate of fiddlesticks!" said the Pine, impatiently. "You are very much behind the times, my friend. Napoleon and Wellington are both only remembered now in histories, and people have other things to do besides quarrelling about which was the greater."

"Oh, cruel, cruel!" wailed the Willow. "To think that my hero should be only remembered in histories! Oh, how my sisters must weep across his tomb!"

"But they don't," said the Pine. "At least, if they do, it is over an empty tomb, for his body was moved to France years and years ago, after lying for nearly twenty years in your island home of St. Helena."

"Is that true?" asked the Willow.

"Yes, of course it is, and you yourself are probably the only one of your family that now bends across a hero's grave."

"I bend across a hero's grave. What do you mean? There are no heroes in Australia," said the Willow, quite forgetting to wail.

"Oh, aren't there? There may be no great and greedy soldier heroes, but I tell you that Australia has known some brave heroes in its time."

"Tell us about them," said the Oak, bending forward with interest. "I have never heard of them either."

"Of course you haven't," said the Pine. "You have always been so occupied in looking down on this new land, and in thinking about your dead hero, that you haven't had time to hear what has been getting on around you. And you too," turning to the Willow—"you have sobbed and sighed for years about your hero's tomb, while all the time the bones of a great, brave gentleman have been lying there beneath your shade."

"Where?" asked the Will ow and Oak together.

"There, on that little island in the pond, underneath

that white obelisk, lies all that is mortal of the man that you and I and all our brothers should count among the greatest of men—Allan Cunningham. He was a man, if you like. He did not spend his days in killing men, and burning towns, and making the whole world tremble with fear. Not he. But he fought enemies just as strong and fierce -heat and thirst in the lonely Australian desert. And why? Not to break down empires, and get great gain for himself; not to wear a golden crown and be bowed down to as a king. But to add to the store of the world's knowledge, to give wisdom to many, to find out the truth about this new and wonderful land, and to teach mankind what he could about Australia's trees and flowers. This is what that man fought, and lived, and died for!"

The Pine's voice rose higher and higher as he spoke till he ended in a triumphant shout, that made the Cygnets tremble with excitement.

"That man," went on the Pine, "has done more for us trees than any of your Napoleons and Wellingtons, and he is the great man you should mourn."

"But he wasn't a soldier," protested the Oak.

"No, he wasn't a soldier, but if you listened to what was going on in the world, instead of always living in the past, you would know that the great man of to-day is not the one who breaks down, but the one who builds up. And a man who adds one new truth to the knowledge of the world, does more for mankind than any soldier who kills and destroys and plunders."

The Willow's tears had dried as she listened to the Pine's words, and she raised her face to him and said— "I like what you say about building up. It is very much better than breaking down."

"Of course it is," said the Pine gently. "I have lived in these gardens for nearly a century. I came from an island far away in the eastern ocean, and I was planted here by the greatest lady in the land. I have seen many, many changes in my life, but I have not spent my time in sighing for my native land, or for that gentle lady. I have always looked upwards, and thought of the future and the good time to come. And so I have grown straight and strong, and now children say I am nearly as tall as the sky. So long as you look backward you will keep going downward. 'Forward' is the right motto for a tree, just as it is for a man."

"I did not think there could be a tree with so much wisdom in a new country," said the Oak, admiringly.

The Pine laughed good-naturedly. "There are many good things in this land for which the people of the old world do not give us credit. But we don't worry if they don't appreciate us yet. They will some day. They have their dreams of a past glory, but we have our hopes of a future!"

The Pine lifted his face proudly as he spoke, and the first rays of the rising sun touched his head with a crown of gold.

Out of the distance came the morning song of the Jacky Winter, the first bird to greet the day. "Sweeter, sweeter, sweeter!" he called, and his voice was full of hope for the future.

The little Cygnets lifted their heads from their mother's wings to look at the Norfolk Island Pine. But he had gone as noiselessly as he had come, and all they saw was that the rising sun shone across the Willow and the Oak, both bending reverently towards the white obelisk on the island.

THE BIRDS' CHRISTMAS TREE

Up on the highland it was very, very hot, but down in the great deep gully, where the tree ferns spread their fronds, where the tall coachwoods reared their heads, and where the staghorns made strange faces on the tree trunks, it was beautifully cool. Down the side of the huge overhanging rock the falls were running with a splash, the very sound of which was enough to make one forget the heat, while the little stream, that ran and gurgled over the rocks, sang a song of coolness.

It was an ideal situation for a party, and so the birds had chosen it as the best place for their Christmas tree. They had picked a spot deep down in the valley, away from the made tracks, where they would not be disturbed by Humans. It was the first time they had ever had a Christmas tree, and they were all very excited about it. The idea had been suggested by the Parrot, who had once lived in a cage for a few months, and had learned a lot about the ways of Humans. He had hated the cage, and had flown away at the first chance, but there was one thing belonging to the Humans of which he had approved, and that was a Christmas tree.

When he first went back to his home in the gully, he used to entertain all the birds he knew with stories of his adventures. He told them how he was caught, and how he had been treated. He told them also of the queer animals that lived with the Humans—cats and dogs and horses—and the little birds would shiver with fright when he talked of how the cats caught and killed sparrows. But the story that all the birds loved best to hear was the one about the Christmas tree. They were never tired of listening to the story, and the Parrot was never tired of telling it. So, when one day a little bird said wistfully, "I wish I could be caught and taken to see a Christmas tree," and several others echoed his words, the Parrot said suddenly: "Why should you be captured to see one? Why shouldn't we have one of our own?"

"One of our own?" repeated the others, "how could we?"

"I don't quite know how we could do it, but I'm sure we could," said the Parrot; "let us all think about it."

So they thought and thought, and at last, with one suggestion and then another, they saw how it could be managed. And when Christmas Day arrived, everything had been thought out, and all was ready.

Only the eldest birds had taken part in the preparations, for, as the Parrot told them that no Human children knew anything about the Christmas tree until it was ready, they had told the baby birds nothing. But the babies knew that something unusual was going to happen, and they were just as excited as their parents.

On the morning of the great day, all the birds in the valley were up at first sign of daylight. Invitations had been sent out to all the parent birds in the valley; they were all coming, and best of all, were bringing their children. Such a chirping and chattering there was from one end of the valley to the other, as the youngsters were being dressed up for the party, for everyone wanted to look his best, and—above all—everyone wanted to be early. The mothers were smoothing their children's feathers, and preening out their own, and saying, "Chut, chut, you children, do keep yourselves tidy!" while the fathers were fussing round saying "Hurry up, hurry up, or we'll be late." But at last, even the biggest family was ready, and they were all off on their way to the party.

The birds who had had charge of the preparations were acting as the hosts, and they were assembled under a canopy of tree ferns to greet their visitors. There were the Cockatoo, the Lyre Bird, the Grey Magpie, the Parrot, the Satin Bird, the little Rock Warbler, and the Dollar Bird, and they all sat side by side, in a row on a branch. Some of the birds had objected to the Lyre Bird being asked, for fear he should mock them and make fun of them. But the Parrot told them that Humans were never unkind to each other at Christmas time, and so they must not keep the Lyre Bird out. And as the Lyre Bird had been very nice and friendly lately, the others agreed to his being invited to take part. So he was one of the hosts.

The first birds to arrive were the Robins. There were four kinds of them, and they wore different coloured waistcoats to distinguish them. Some wore scarlet vests, some rose-pink, some bright yellow, others flame-coloured; and they were all so beautiful that it was hard to say which looked the best. They were all gentle little fellows, and hopped along in a happy, friendly way, without any fuss.

But the next arrivals made up in fuss what they lacked in colour. These were the Scrub-wrens and little Tits, who all came together, chattering and scolding at their children and making quite a commotion.

Next came the Parrakeets—gaily coloured birds with loud screeching voices—and they shrieked and screamed at each other, as if they were very cross, though they were really quite friendly.

Then came many other birds—Blue Jays, Woodswallows, Mountain Thrushes, Pilot-birds, Flycatchers, and—last of all—the Raven, the Hawk, and the Butcher Bird.

At the sight of the last two there was a great fluster amongst the small birds, and they began to scream and fly about in a frightened way, although neither the Hawk nor the Butcher Bird attempted to touch them. But the Parrot called out in a loud voice—"Don't be afraid, little ones. The Hawk and the Butcher Bird are no longer your enemies, Christmas is the time when all Humans love each other, and would not do anything cruel, and so, as we are copying their Christmas tree, we are also going to copy their manners, and every bird is kind and friendly to-day."

At the Parrot's words the little birds grew quieter, and when the Raven, the Hawk, and the Butcher Bird said—"Hear, hear, we agree to that," and the other birds all applauded, the little ones joined in and shouted "hooray" as loudly as the rest.

"Now as we are all here," said the Parrot, "we may as well go into the other bower where the tree is."

"But evidently we are not all here," said the Grey Magpie, "for I see someone coming now. See there."

They looked to where he pointed, and there was a sleepy bird coming slowly through the trees.

"It's the Boobook Owl," said the Hawk. "You might

expect him to be late."

Just as he spoke, the Boobook Owl sat down on a tree, and settled himself as if he meant to stay there.

"Why, he's going to sleep!" said the Parrot in disgust. "Someone had better call him."

"Come, come, come!" shrieked the Grey Magpie.

"Come along, come along," screamed the Black Magpie.

"Come at once, will you; ah, will you?" screeched the Black Cockatoo.

As they all called together the noise was almost deafening, and it quite woke the Boobook Owl. He left the tree he was on, and came up to where the others were assembled.

He was a streaky, brown bird, with big yellow eyes, and he said in a sleepy, complaining voice, "Why ever did you have the party so early?"

"Early!" exclaimed the Parrot, "why the sun's been up for ages."

"Yes, but the moon's only just gone down, and I haven't had any sleep."

"You shouldn't stay out all night, and you wouldn't be so sleepy in the morning," said the Grey Magpie sternly.

"That's all very well for you," said the Boobook Owl, yawning, "but I can't catch things in the daylight."

"Well, don't let us waste any more time in discussion," said the Parrot. "Everything is ready, so we may as well proceed to the party. Lyre Bird, will you lead the way?"

The Lyre Bird bowed low, then, spreading out his tail, proudly walked towards the entrance of the bower where the Christmas tree stood. The Parrot and Black Cockatoo came next, then the Grey Magpie, and the little Rock Warbler, and after them the Dollar Bird and the Satin Bird walked. The other birds fell in behind their hosts, and the long procession filed into the bower.

And, oh, what a sight was there! In the centre of the clearing stood a tall, slim young tree, which was laden with masses of brilliant Christmas Bush and bunches of Christmas Bells, which tinkled in the gentle breeze. Hanging on every branch were numbers of mysterious green bags, made of coachwood leaves sewn together, and ornamented with moss; and little dishes made of interwoven ferns were firmly fixed in the forks of the branches.

As each pair of birds entered the bower, and saw this wonderful sight they exclaimed aloud: "Oh, how beautiful!" and the children were so eager to get near the tree, that they all fell over each other, and rolled about the ground with a nice fluttering of wings, till their mothers picked them up, and told them to be good.

The Parrot was very proud and pleased when he saw how the birds admired the Christmas tree, for though the other hosts had helped him, he had planned all the arrangements for the decorations, and the tree was as much like a Human's as it could be.

"So you really like it?" he said, when all the visitors had walked round and round the tree, and duly admired it.

"Like it?" exclaimed the Blue Jay, "why it's just perfect. Three cheers for the Parrot;" and all the others joined in, till the valley rang with their "hurrahs!"

The Parrot smiled and bowed, and then he and the other hosts sat down in a row beside the tree, and the rest of the company seated themselves all round the bower, waiting expectantly for what was to happen next.

When they were all comfortably arranged the Parrot

addressed them:

"When Humans have a Christmas tree," he said, "it is the custom to sing a carol before they distribute the presents. So we have written a song which the Thunder Bird has consented to sing, and we want you all to join in the chorus."

A beautiful bird with a yellow breast, white throat, and black collar, hopped up on to a ferntree frond, and in a rich, clear voice, sang this song:

> Christmas comes but once a year,
> You will hear all Humans say,
> And when it comes it brings good cheer,
> Hate and envy die away.
> Christmas is a happy day,
> Hate and envy die away.
>
> Friendship lives in every heart,
> And the earth is filled with peace;
> Kind thoughts from each breast do start,
> Quarrellings and anger cease.
> Christmas is a happy day,
> Hate and envy die away.
>
> Not alone are Humans kind
> On this happy Christmas day;
> All the birds, too, you will find
> Friendly, loving, happy, gay.
> Christmas is a happy day,
> Hate and envy die away.

All the birds joined in the chorus and looked very happy as they sang. Even the Hawk and Butcher Bird joined in the singing, and looked quite soft and friendly, and not a bit fierce.

"Now," said the Parrot, "we must distribute the presents. Satin and Dollar, will you begin?"

The Satin Bird went to one side of the tree, making his queer noise like the sound of satin being torn. He was a lovely bird in his full grownup dress of rich dark blue, and he made a pretty contrast to the red of the Christmas Bush. The Dollar Bird flew to the other side of the tree, and as he spread his blue wings, two round silver spots could be plainly seen.

"It is those spots which give him his name of Dollar Bird," explained a mother Scrub-wren to her son. "They are just like dollars or crowns."

"Then I suppose his children are called half-crowns?" said a little Tit, which set all the other little birds giggling.

But there wasn't much time to laugh at a silly little Tit's jokes, for the presents were being handed round, and the young birds could think of nothing else. The Satin and Dollar Birds handed them down from the tree, and the Lyre Bird, Black Cockatoo, and Grey Magpie carried them round, while the Parrot and Rock Warbler sat and watched the fun.

There were presents for all. The mysterious green bags, which had caused much wonder, contained little flies and dainty insects, such as all the smaller birds loved. On the fern leaf dishes were heaps of grubs and worms for some of the larger birds, and fruit and berries for the Parrot, the Parrakeets, the Grey Magpie and the Satin Bird, who are all vegetarians. Everyone received what he most liked, and they were all just going to begin to enjoy the feast, when a sleepy voice said: "Where's my present?"

It was the Boobook Owl. He had gone to sleep while they were singing, and had just awakened, and was very sleepy and cross. All the hosts looked at one another in consternation. They had quite forgotten the Boobook Owl, and had prepared no present for him. What should they do?

"I want my present," said the Boobook Owl, peevishly. "Where's my present?"

The Parrot quickly put some of his fruit and berries on to a leaf, and passed them to the Boobook, saying: "Will you have some fruit?"

"No," said the Boobook Owl crossly, "you know very well I don't eat fruit. I want a mouse. I never came to such a stupid party!"

The poor Parrot looked terribly worried. He had wanted everyone to be happy, and now here was someone as cross as could be, saying the party was stupid.

"Whatever shall we do?" he asked the Grey Magpie.

"Take no notice of him, and perhaps he will go to sleep again," said the Grey Magpie.

But the Boobook Owl was wide awake now, and meant to stay so. He was very hungry and very cross, and he began to cry in a peevish tone— "More pork, more pork."

"Oh, what can we give him? We haven't any pork," said the Parrot.

"Mice will do," said the Boobook Owl, who had heard his remark.

"But we haven't any mice," exclaimed the Parrot impatiently, at which the Boobook Owl began to wail again—

"More pork, more pork."

"Oh, this is terrible. He is spoiling the party. We'll have to put him out," said the Grey Magpie, but he was interrupted by a whirring noise, and the Hawk swooped suddenly past him. There was a shriek of fright from the little birds, but the Hawk went straight past them, and swept down on to a tree beyond the bower. In a moment he returned and in his claw was a mouse.

"Here," he said, throwing it down in front of the Boobook Owl, "take the mouse and stop your wailing."

The Boobook Owl's big yellow eyes opened wide with amazement. "I never thought to see a Hawk give food to any other bird," he said at last.

"The Parrot says that Christmas is a time for giving, and I want to be like the others," said the Hawk gruffly as he went hack to his place next to the Butcher Bird, while the Boobook Owl began to greedily gobble up the mouse.

"Bravo!" cried the Parrot. "I'm proud of you, friend Hawk."

"So am I," called the Thunder Bird, and he at once began to sing:

"The Hawk, once fiercest bird of prey,
Now gentle is as any dove,
Because he's learned that Christmas Day
Is meant for love."

"Very nice, indeed, Thunder Bird," cried several birds, while the Hawk tried to look unconscious, pretending he wasn't at all pleased with this praise.

"Now," said the Parrot, "I think we had better have

games, for that is what Humans do. But, perhaps you would like to dance?"

"Yes, yes, a dance, a dance," was the cry.

So they cleared a space in the centre, and the Lyre Bird and Satin Bird performed several dances, whilst the others whistled the tune. When the dance was finished, the beautiful black-faced Flycatcher gave an exhibition of catching flies on the wing, which was much applauded.

In the midst of the applause came a sudden shriek. A young Scrub-wren had been leaning too far forward to see the performance, and had overbalanced and fallen. Before she could pick herself up, the Butcher Bird darted towards her. The Scrub-wren saw him coming, and shrieked with terror, cowering down on the ground. All the other small birds joined the screaming, and some shouted "Bully, bully!"

"Cowardy custard!" But the Butcher Bird took no notice, but swept straight past them down on the Scrub-wren.

Then a marvellous thing happened. Instead of killing the smaller bird, as everyone expected, the Butcher Bird gently picked her up, and placed her on the twig beside her mother, saying, "Don't be frightened, little one," while all the company stared in wonder.

"The Parrot said we all had to be kind to each other at Christmas time, and I didn't want to hurt the little silly," explained the Butcher Bird in answer to their looks of surprise.

"Truly, this Christmas is a wonderful thing," said the Black Cockatoo, "if it can make the Hawk and Butcher Bird gentle to others. Sing us something about the Butcher Bird, Mister Thunder Bird."

"With pleasure," said the Thunder Bird, and he sang:

The Butcher Bird
Once brutal was,
And killed the smaller birds;
But now you've seen
Him help the Wren,
With tender, loving words.

"That's true, that's true!" shouted the little birds, while the Butcher Bird blushed with pleasure.

By this time the Boobook Owl had finished gobbling up his mouse, and being less hungry, was prepared to be interested in the doings of the others.

"What is this Christmas time of which you're all talking?" he asked the Blue Jay, who sat next him.

"The Parrot says it is the time of the year when everyone is kind to everyone else," replied the Jay.

"He says that Humans are all thoughtful and unselfish, and have more pleasure in giving presents than in receiving them."

"But why should they?" asked the Boo book Owl. "Only silly people would give away things when they could keep them for themselves. I'm sure I wouldn't give anything away that I wanted—Christmas or no Christmas."

"Then you're very selfish," said the Blue Jay, moving away in disgust.

"Mister Parrot," called the Boobook Owl, "I don't think much of this plan of yours for us all to give presents. I suppose you would like us to give them all to you."

Several birds cried "Shame!" and the Parrot looked very grieved as he replied sternly—"You approved of the plan when the Hawk gave you the mouse he might have kept for himself."

The Boobook Owl looked a little ashamed, as he said—"Oh, but that's different."

"Of course you think it is different. But why should the Hawk be kind to you if you are unkind to others? You are not a friend of his, and yet he caught and gave you a mouse, without which you would have gone hungry."

"It was very kind of him," said the Boobook Owl, who was really not a bad fellow at heart, though he was stupid in the daytime. "There must be something in Christmas if it makes the Hawk kind to other birds."

"There is a great deal in Christmas," said the Parrot. "It fills everyone's heart with love, and that is the best thing in the world. You are the only bird here to-day who is not friendly and kind to the others."

"I don't want to be the only one," said the Boobook Owl in his wailing voice. "I want to be like the others."

At that moment a little mouse ran out just under his nose. For a second the Owl gazed hungrily at it, then he turned to the Parrot, and said- "It would be cruel to kill him, when I am not hungry, wouldn't it?"

"Yes, it would," agreed the Parrot, looking very happy at the Boobook Owl's words, and all the others laughed and said—"The Boobook Owl is kind at last. He is no longer greedy," whereupon the Thunder Bird jumped up again on to the fern tree, and sang:

In days gone by the Boobook Owl
Would wail and whine, and scold and scowl
Would kill a mouse and eat him up,
And then want more on which to sup.

But now you see, no longer shy,
The little mice go skipping by.
The Owl is kind, no fear have they,
For love rules all on Christmas Day.

Then the Lyre Bird flew up on to the Christmas tree, and said: "My friends, I think you will all agree that the Christmas tree has been a great success. We have all been very happy to-day, and now the sun is sinking, and it will soon be time to go home; but before we go, I want to thank the Parrot for telling us about this wonderful Christmas time, which makes us all so kind to each other, and then I want you all to join in the song I am going to sing. But first, three cheers for the Parrot."

"Hooray, hooray, hooray!" cried all the birds again and again. And then the Lyre Bird sang in a rich ringing voice—

Christmas day is over,
Happy, happy day.
Homeward now you're going,
Flying far away.

But you will remember
That to-day has been
Full of love and friendship,
Happiness serene.

Big birds helping small ones,
Kindness between all,
Thus the Christmas feeling
Comes to great and small.

Let us keep this feeling
Through the coming year,
Tenderness and kindness
Banish every fear.

And "a merry Christmas,"
As the Humans say,
Let us wish each other,
Every Christmas day.

One after another the birds took it up, and large and small, young and old, sang with all their might, till the valley rang with the joyousness of their song, and sent a thrill of Christmas gladness to the hearts of the Humans on the highlands.

THE LITTLE BLACK DUCK

ON THE island in the Zoological Gardens there once lived a young Black Duck. He was a very happy little fellow, and although he lived in a little island in the middle of a little pond, he was quite content with his surroundings, for he had been born on this island, and had lived there all his short life.

As is often the way with people who have seen only one place in their lives, he thought the island was the most beautiful spot in the world. He also thought that the high iron fence which surrounds the Zoo was the end of the world, and that there was nothing beyond it. He knew that upon the hillside there lived lions and tigers and bears, and other terrible wild animals, for he had often heard them roar; and the sparrows, which flew about all over the Gardens, had told him of the wonderful birds and beasts which lived there; so he was very glad he lived on the island in the pond.

All the other birds on the island had one wing cut to prevent them from flying away, but the little Black Duck was so satisfied with his surroundings that his wings had not been clipped; and the other birds all envied him, for they did not love the place as he did, but longed to fly away.

"It's well to be you," said a Curlew, who had recently

been brought to the island. "I only wish I had your luck and my two wings; I know I wouldn't stay here very long."

"What would you do?" asked the Black Duck.

"I should fly away to the end of the world, far, far away from this hateful island."

The Black Duck was amazed. He could not understand this strange, sad bird, who called his beautiful island "hateful," and wanted to be at the end of the world.

"But it's not safe to be at the end of the world," he said.

"Why not?" asked the Curlew.

"Because there are lions and tigers there."

"Not in the parts I came from. There are no animals there but kangaroos and opossums, and dear little native bears, and none of them would hurt you."

"Yes, the sparrows told me about them, but there are lions and tigers there, too."

"Well, I never saw them, and I never heard of them being there. But have you been out West yourself?"

"No," said the Black Duck. "I was born on the island, and I have never been beyond the pond."

"Born on this island!" exclaimed the Curlew. "And never been beyond the pond! Oh, you poor thing!"

The Black Duck did not quite understand the Curlew, for he could see nothing remarkable about being born on the island, and certainly that was no reason for calling him a "poor thing." Still, he was too good-tempered to be annoyed with the Curlew's remarks, so he replied:

"I am very fond of the island and the pond, and am glad I was born here. But where were you born?"

The Curlew looked very sad at this question, and, lifting his long bill into the air, he gazed across the gardens and replied mournfully:

"Oh, far, far away from here. Quite at the other end of the world."

"Perhaps you will forget all about the place where you were born when you know the island better," the Black Duck said, hoping to cheer the Curlew.

But the Curlew did not answer. He was still gazing pensively into the distance, and seemed to have forgotten his companion. So, after waiting a few minutes, the Black Duck left him to himself, and walked off to find a more cheerful companion to have a game with him.

There were plenty of other birds about, and he asked one after another to come and play, but none of them would. Some were too lazy, some too tired, and some too old; so the Black Duck could not find a playmate.

"Oh, well," he said to himself, "if no one will play with me, I suppose I must have a nap to pass the time." He had just tucked his head into his back, and was going to sleep, when he was aroused by a great whirring of wings.

Instantly he was wide awake, and looked round to see what was making all this noise. It was a number of tall, grey birds with long legs. They had just been let loose on the island by the keepers, and they were making a great commotion on finding themselves in a strange place.

The other birds were all aroused, too, and gathered round the new arrivals, for most of them had seen the same kind of tall grey birds before. But the Black Duck stood where he was, and stared with amazement. Never had he seen such tall birds with such long legs. Most of the birds on the island were very little bigger than himself, but these new-comers seemed nearly as tall as trees.

"What are they?" he asked the Curlew, who had just come up beside him.

"They're Brolgas, or as some Mortals sometimes call them, 'Native Companions.'"

"Where do they come from?"

"From my country, out back."

"Is that at the end of the world?" asked the Black Duck.

"Yes, miles and miles away from here," and the Curlew went on to greet the new-comers.

In a few days the Brolgas were as much at home on the island as the other birds, but they were not at all contented, for they also had one wing cut. This was very noticeable in their case, because of the habit they had of stretching out their wings when they wanted to dance, as they often did. The clipped wings spoilt their beauty, and several of the birds made remarks about them.

"It's a cruel shame," cried the Curlew, "that we who want to fly away should all have our wings cut, and that silly little Black Duck, who is quite content to stay here, should have two whole wings."

At this, all the Brolgas turned and looked at the Black Duck.

"Do you mean to say," said one of them, "that you have two whole wings, and yet you are satisfied to stay here, in this awful place?"

"It's not an awful place," said the Black Duck, who was growing tired of hearing his home abused; "it's the most beautiful spot in the world."

All the other birds laughed scornfully, and the Curlew said: "He thinks it is the most beautiful place in the world because he's never been anywhere else."

The Brolgas opened their mouths in amazement, then walked round the Black Duck, staring at him as if they had never seen such a creature before. When they had all walked round, and looked well at him, one said: "Are you really a Black Duck?"

"Of course I am," replied the Black Duck, who was beginning to be annoyed. "And you have never been anywhere except on this island and pond?"

"No," said the Black Duck, shortly.

"Oh, you poor thing, you poor thing!" and all the Brolgas shook their heads sadly.

"I'm not a poor thing," said the Black Duck, angrily; "and I'll thank you not to call me names."

But the Brolgas just shook their heads again, and altogether repeated: "A Black Duck! Poor thing, poor thing!"

By this time the Black Duck was very angry, and he shouted at them:

"At any rate, this pond and island are better than the old iron fence at the end of the world where you came from."

"Old iron fence?" repeated the Brolgas. "What do you mean?"

"The Curlew said you came from the end of the world."

"Well, what if we did?"

"You know very well that is the end of the world," said the Black Duck pointing with one wing to the iron fence.

For a minute the birds all looked at each other in amazement; then there came such a burst of laughter as had never been heard in that place before. All the birds on the island joined in it, and the place echoed with the noise. All laughed, but the Black Duck. He could see nothing to laugh at, and was furious with the others.

At last the Curlew was able to speak, and, pointing to the Black Duck, said: "He thinks these Gardens are the whole world, and that the old iron fence is the end of the world. I see now why he said there were lions and tigers at the end of the world," and again he went off into a shriek of laughter, in which all the others joined.

"Do you mean to say you have never flown across the wide plains?" said one Brolga.

"Never swam upon the western waterholes?" said another.

"Never played amongst the cool swaying reeds?" asked a third.

"No," shouted the Black Duck; "and I don't want to."

"Oh, poor thing, poor thing," said all the Brolgas together, shaking their heads from side to side.

The Black Duck could stand no more.

"You just leave off calling me a poor thing," he shouted. "You think you're very fine because you've got such long legs and long necks. Pooh, propsticks!" and with this he waddled off to the water as fast as he could.

For a minute the Brolgas were too surprised to do anything, for no one had ever thought the little Black Duck could be so cross. Then one of them calling out, "I'll punish you for your impudence," darted off after the Duck.

By this time the Black Duck had reached the water, and the Brolga waded in after him. The little bird waited until the large one came quite close, and then, calling out "Catch me if you can," whirred off across to the other side of the pond.

Again the Brolga darted after him, and once more the Black Duck waited till he came up; then, shouting out, "Pooh, propsticks!" he again whirred away, rippling the water as he went. This went on for some time, the Brolga making futile darts, and the black Duck mocking his pursuer, till at last the Brolga, in disgust, gave up the chase and stalked back to his friends.

Now, though the Black Duck had been so angry with the Brolgas, he had heard what they said about the wide plains and western waterholes and cool swaying reeds, and these names awakened in his heart a queer feeling which he could not understand. All of a sudden he had ceased to be satisfied with the pond and the island, and he began to wonder if there really might be something beyond the iron fence. All the birds had laughed so much at him for thinking it was the end of the world, that he felt they must know something of other places.

He was too indignant to go near the others for a while, and so kept quite by himself. But he soon grew tired of his own company, and did want to hear about those plains and waterholes. He was afraid to go near the Brolgas after the names he had called them, but he remembered his old friend the Curlew had said he came from the same country; he, therefore, thought he would ask him about it.

So he went over to where the Curlew was standing alone, and said in a meek little voice, "Good morning, Curlew."

The Curlew turned and looked at him, saying, "Oh, it's you, is it? Have you got over your sulks?"

"I wasn't sulky," said the Black Duck; "I was only angry with you all for laughing at me."

"Well, no wonder we laughed. How could we help it when you were so silly? To think the old iron fence was the end of the world!" and the Curlew laughed again at the thought.

"Well, no one ever told me there was anything outside," said the Black Duck, sadly; "and it was as far as I could see. How could I know?"

"There's something in that," said the Curlew. "Perhaps we shouldn't have laughed at you so much. We should have remembered you were young and ignorant."

"Well, what is there outside the fence?" asked the Black Duck

"What is there? Why the whole world. This is only a tiny, tiny speck, and outside that fence there is everything—plains, rivers, mountains, and seas."

"Tell me about the plains," said the Black Duck eagerly, "and about the western waterholes."

So the Curlew told him about the western plains where he had been born. He told him how they stretched for miles and miles, and how the rivers ran across them; he told him of the trees that grew along the rivers' banks, and of the marshes where the reeds grow green and long, and where the wild fowl love to play.

"There are thousands of your brothers out there," he said to the Black Duck, "and they fly about all over the country. That is why the Brolgas could not understand your wanting to stay here when you could fly away to the plains. And that is why they called you a 'poor thing.'"

The Black Duck was silent. Again that queer feeling was at his heart, and it made him very sad. After a while he asked the Curlew: "If I flew away from here, do you think I could find my way to the western plains?"

"You might meet some of your brothers going there, for I often see them flying overhead."

"Do you think they would show me the way?"

"Yes, I am quite sure they would," replied the Curlew. "You are very silly not to go."

"I think I shall wait till I am a little older," said the Black Duck, nervously. "You see, I have never been beyond this pond."

"No, and you're not likely to, if you are afraid to venture," answered the Curlew, stalking off.

The Black Duck thought seriously over these last words of the Curlew's, and wondered if he were silly to stay, or whether it would be rash to go. Sometimes he thought he would fly away at once; then he felt nervous, and decided that the pond and the island were good enough for him. And so the days passed, and he was still in the same place.

Each day, as it came, was hotter than the last, for the summer was coming, and the birds all round talked of the places they had come from, of the plains, and rivers, and trees, till they were all as homesick as they could be. And the little Black Duck was also homesick, though he did not know it, for he could think of nothing but those plains and western waterholes.

At last, one day the heat was so intense that it was almost unbearable. The pond water was quite warm, and not at all refreshing, and there was scarcely any shade. The little Black Duck felt wretched and tired, so going to his friend the Curlew he asked him to talk about the plains.

"What is the use of telling you about them?" grumbled the Curlew. "You don't care about them. If you did, you would not stay here when you could fly away to them."

"I do want to go," said the Black Duck. "But, oh, I am so frightened I should lose my way. If only I could see my brothers!"

"Look, look!" cried the Curlew, excitedly. "Look up there."

The Black Duck gazed up into the sky, and there was a V-shaped flock of birds flying across it; tiny black specks they seemed, but the sight of them made the Black Duck tremble, he knew not why.

"What are they?" he asked breathlessly.

"Your brothers!" cried the Curlew. "Now is your chance. Go, you silly fellow; go quickly!"

"Will they know me?"

"Yes, yes. Oh, be quick, or you'll lose them," and, unable to restrain his impatience, the Curlew gave the Black Duck a poke with his long bill.

But it wasn't needed. At last the Black Duck had made up his mind. with a flap he rose from the ground, and shouting out, "I'm going, I'm going," flew quickly away, up, up, up, higher and higher, till the pond and the island were far beneath him, and he could no longer see the Curlew.

Before him flew that double line of dark specks which he knew were his brothers, and he called with a loud voice:

"Wait for me, brothers, wait for me!"

The flying line heard him, halted, then wheeled towards him, and in a moment he was in their midst, feeling the coolness of the air as it was fanned by their wings.

Then on again they flew, across the land. Far below he could see blue water flashing in the sunlight, and dark trees, promising coolness and shade. But still the flock went on, till the sea was left behind, and tall mountains rose up before them. The air grew cooler and lighter here, but the birds did not stay. Across the mountains they went, on and on, till they came to a wide river with green rushes and bending trees, while far on either side stretched vast plains. Then, with a whirr, like the sound of rushing wind, the flock of ducks swept down on to the river. At last the Black Duck was in his own country.

And there he spent many happy days, swimming amongst the waving reeds, and flying across the open plains. Often he thought of his friends in the Zoo, and sometimes he thought he would go back just to tell them that he had learned that they were right, and that there were many more beautiful places in the world than the little island and pond; but then he remembered that all the birds there had their wings clipped, and that if he went back his would he cut too. So he stayed where he was, and lived happily for many, many years.

THE PROPER WAY

The young Dottrel wanted to build a nest, but did not know how to begin. He had been in the world just a year, and had spent most of his time running about the sand, catching little crabs and worms and other things good to eat. But now that the Spring had come, and all the other birds were making nests, he felt that he would like to build a home for himself and his little wife; and as he did not know how to begin, he looked round for someone who could tell him.

Behind him, amongst the trees in the bush, he could hear many birds talking and calling to each other, as they flew about collecting material for their new homes. The Dottrel did not know any of the bush birds, but as they sounded so friendly and happy, he thought they would not mind giving him a little information. So he ran across the sand and through the grass at the edge of the lagoon where he lived, and entered the bush.

Here he found hundreds of birds, of all sizes and colours, flying busily about. They took no notice of him as he ran along the ground towards them, but, as they did not seem unfriendly, he was not very shy. He looked round to see which bird he should speak to first, but, before he could open his beak to address anyone, he heard a voice behind him say: "Hullo, my young friend! What are you doing here?"

The Dottrel turned to look at the speaker, and found it was the Red-bill, a bird he knew quite well by sight, for he lived in the reeds on the edge of the swamp. He was quite pleased to see a familiar face and said:—"I have come to ask how to build a nest."

"How to build a nest?" repeated the Red-bill. "Why, that's quite easy. You just get a few reeds and twist them round and fix them in a clump of grass, and your nest is built."

"It sounds easy," said the Dottrel, "but where do you get the reeds?"

"Oh, break them off, or pull them up with your beak."

The Dottrel looked at the Red-bill's big, strong beak, and, thinking of his own, which was slim and slender, he replied doubtfully—"I am afraid my beak is not strong enough to break reeds."

"No, it doesn't look fit for much," agreed the Red-bill. "Why don't you make it grow?"

"Is that the only way to build a nest?" asked the Dottrel, ignoring the Red-bill's question.

"The only proper way," replied the other with dignity, as he stalked away.

"What's that I hear?" asked a small bird with a long, sharp beak, that came swiftly darting towards the Dottrel at that moment. "What did Red-bill say was the only proper way?"

"He said that the only proper way to build a nest was to break off reeds and twist them in and out."

"Twisted reeds!" said the other scornfully. "Why, whoever wants to build a nest of reeds?"

"I don't," said the Dottrel.

"I should think not," said the other, who was a Honey-eater. "No sensible bird does. The right way to make a nest is to get little roots and fibres, and threads of plants, and weave them into a basket hanging on two twigs."

"That sounds very pretty," said the Dottrel admiringly, "but the grasses which grow on the sand where I live are so stiff that I don't think they would twist into a basket."

"You should look for other grass then," said the Honey-eater, "for that is certainly the best way to build a nest. It is so cosy, and when the wind blows it is like being in a swing."

"Don't you take any notice of what he says," interrupted a tiny green bird with a red head, who had come up unnoticed. "Don't you build a nest like his, or you will rock right out when the wind blows. You build a long nest like mine where you can sit deep down at the bottom, and nothing can turn you out."

The speaker was the Redhead, and he was so fussy and self-important that the Dottrel was quite impressed.

"That certainly sounds safer," he agreed. "Of course it is," said the Redhead. "Why, there isn't a nest in the bush as safe as mine!"

"Your nest safe?" exclaimed a Jacky Winter, who had flown up to hear what was being said. "Why there isn't a nest in the bush that's easier to see. Even the smallest boy can see it. The proper way to build a nest," he added, turning to the Dottrel, "is to make a tiny little cup of a nest on the fork of a branch. Then no one will see it, for it is too small!"

"Yes, that ought to be safe," said the Dottrel admiringly,

"for I can understand that a boy would not easily see a nest as small as that."

"No, but he would see your tail sticking over the edge," cried a Native Canary, who had joined the group.

The Dottrel looked worried, as he said: "Of course, if a nest were too small, there wouldn't be much room to sit."

"Of course there wouldn't," agreed the Native Canary. "And it is silly to have a nest that your head and tail stick out of. Now, the proper way to make a nest is to cover it all over, with just a hole in the side where you can slip in and out without being seen."

"What a horrible, stuffy idea!" cried a Fantail. "It's quite hot enough as it is, without burying oneself in a nest like that. The way I build a nest is like this. I make it round and open, with a chimney underneath to keep me cool," and she fanned herself with her outspread tail, exclaiming, "How hot it is!"

The Dottrel looked at her with admiration. "I would like a house with a chimney underneath," he said. "Of what do you make it?"

"Cobweb and stuff. Cobweb makes such a nice soft covering, just like kid"

"Yes," broke in a little Tree-runner sarcastically, "and as all boys know that kid grows on trees, they, of course, never think it is a nest. The proper way to make a nest is to put it in the fork of a branch, and cover it with the bark of the tree. Then anyone who sees it, thinks it is just part of the branch, and walks past."

"I really don't see why you small birds spend so much time in finishing off the outside of your nests," cried a Magpie. "So long as the inside is soft and comfortable, who cares what the outside is like? I build my nest in the quickest way I can, with twigs and sticks, and if people do see, I don't care, for I place it too high for them to reach it. Don't you waste your time finishing off the outside," he said turning to the Dottrel. "I never do."

"Oh, we all know that!" interjected the Peewee. "We all know that you are too untidy to finish off, and you have rough sticks jutting out all over your nest. It's a marvel that your children don't get killed on them when they're trying to leave home. Now the proper way to build a nest is to make it a nice tidy round mud basin. You can easily get the mud anywhere, and there is no need then to fly about all over the country looking for suitable sticks."

"Ha, ha, ha!" laughed the Kookaburra, "it seems to me it wastes as much time carrying mud as sticks." He turned towards the Dottrel as he spoke, and lowering his voice, said confidentially, "Don't you carry the mud. Let the ants do it for you."

"Ants!" repeated the Dottrel in surprise. "What have they to do with it?"

"The White Ants build a big earth nest in a tree, and I go and use it."

"But what becomes of the ants?"

"I eat them!" said the Kookaburra, bursting out laughing.

"Oh! how cruel!"

"It's fun catching them."

"Ugh! I don't like ants, and I couldn't live amongst them, so I don't think I'll make a nest like yours, Mister Kookaburra."

"All the more ants for me, then!" laughed the Kookaburra, as he flew away.

"Why bother about having mud on a tree at all?" asked a Bee-eater, a gorgeously-coloured bird with long tail feathers. "The proper place for mud is on the ground, and that's the best place for a nest. If you take my advice, you will not spend your strength in carrying mud up a tree, but you will dig a hole in a bank of earth, and leave your eggs there."

As he spoke a large ugly bird stalked t'?, and said: "I think there is something very, cowardly in hiding your eggs away in a hole like that. No one can accuse me of being a coward. I build a high mound of leaves and earth and leave my eggs there."

"That's very brave of you," said the Bee-eater, "and it's very kind too. For it must be so convenient for people to find."

"Not at all," said the Brush Turkey, for that was the big bird's name. "Not at all on the contrary, people think it is a mountain,, and walk right round it."

"I'm afraid I could never build anything so large as a mountain," said the Dottrel sadly.

"Don't you try," cried a Parrot cheerfully. "Don't you bother about building mounds or digging holes. You just look round for a nice comfortable hole in the top branch of the highest gum tree you can find, and you wont want anything better. That's the proper way to build a nest.'"

"But I would be frightened to live on the top branch of the highest gum-tree," said the Dottrel, trembling at the thought.

"Well, that's the best advice I can give you," said the Parrot.

"Oh dear, oh dear!" said the Dottrell, "it is very perplexing. You all give me different advice, and each one tells me that his is the proper way of building a nest. Whom am I to believe?"

"Me! Me! Me!" cried each of the birds, shrieking and calling in such confusion that the poor little Dottrel was more bewildered than ever.

In the midst of it all a wailing voice whispered in his ear: "Take my advice. Don't build a nest at all, but put your eggs in the other birds' nests, and that will save you all trouble."

The Dottrel turned and faced the speaker indignantly.

"I know you, you are the Cuckoo," he said. "How dare you suggest anything so mean to me?" he exclaimed. "I may be young and stupid, but I'm not a sneak!"

The Cuckoo hunched his shoulders at the angry words, and skulked away without answering, leaving the Dottrel muttering to himself—"Put my eggs in other birds' nests, indeed! Not build a nest at all, indeed!"

"It's not a bad plan," said a Nightjar, a bird with big round eyes.

"What's not a bad plan?"

"To build no nest at all. I don't, and it saves a lot of trouble."

"But do you put your eggs in other birds' nests?" asked the Dottrel in surprise.

"Oh, no, I leave them on the ground in a sheltered spot and they are quite safe. Why, you could put your eggs on the sand, which they exactly resemble in colour, and no one would ever notice them."

"It would certainly save a lot of worry," said the Dottrel, "but isn't it a very lazy plan?"

"Of course it is," shrieked all the other birds. "You build a mud nest! No, a twig nest! No, a fibre nest! No, a bark nest! No, a reed nest!"

For a few moments the Dottrel was too bewildered to speak. Then suddenly he grew very angry, and pushing through them shouted loudly: "Stop your screaming and yelling! I don't want to know how any of your stupid old nests are made. I don't want a nest at all."

With these words he ran through their midst, and, scuttling over the ground as fast as his legs could carry him, disappeared through the grass at the edge of the lagoon.

And from that day to this he and his wife have never made a nest, but Mrs. Dottrel just leaves her eggs on the sand. And as they are of the same colour as the earth around them, they are as safe as they would be in any nest.

THE LEAF THAT LONGED TO BE RED

THERE WAS once a very discontented Leaf. He lived on a large spreading Sassafras tree in the thick shade of the beautiful brush, where the tall tree-ferns stretched their slender arms towards him, and the maiden-hair ferns grew thick upon the ground. The birds sang in the branches above his head, and the butterflies danced around him. In fact, it was the most delightful place for any leaf to live, and yet this Leaf was as unhappy as if he lived in a city park where the dust soiled and the smoke suffocated.

And the whole reason of his unhappiness was this—he wanted to be red. He was a brilliant shining green, the very prettiest colour a leaf can be, and yet nothing would suit this silly fellow but that he must be red.

He was a very young Leaf, and had been green all his life. He had always been contented until one day some American people had sat beneath his tree and talked, and he heard one say:

"This is a beautiful bit of bush, but what a pity there is no red or yellow to show up the green." And another answered

"Yes, if only there were some red leaves like those on the maples in our country, it would be perfect."

And then they went on to say how pretty red leaves

were, and how nice they were to decorate with, and how sweet they looked in vases on the table, until the Leaf longed to be one of these wonderful red leaves of which people thought so much, and he felt quite sad and miserable that he was just ordinary bright green.

"Do the leaves here never turn red?" asked one of the Americans; and someone answered—

"I believe some do in the autumn, but only a few."

The leaf heard, and in his heart a hope sprang up. Why shouldn't he be one of the few? He was as large as any of his brothers on the tree, and had just as much right to receive this special honour as any other. He made up his mind to find out who turned some of the leaves red, and then to ask if he might be amongst the favoured ones.

So he asked an old Staghorn, which lived close by, who it was that painted the leaves red in the autumn, and the Staghorn replied—

"Mother Nature. She comes with her paint pot in April and May, and dabs a spot of colour here and there, sometimes red and sometimes yellow. But I really think she must love green best of all, for she lets most of the trees remain that colour, I am glad to say she never disturbs my beautiful blue-green leaves with any of her bright paints."

"But wouldn't you like to be red?" asked the Leaf.

"Certainly not," replied the Staghorn. "I am quite satisfied as I am."

But the Leaf was far from being satisfied. All day he wondered when Mother Nature would come, and he was afraid to sleep at night for fear he should miss her, for he intended to ask her to paint him red.

He thought so much about it that he forgot to drink in

the dew and rain, and even forgot to lean forward to catch the sunbeams as they flickered through the tall branches overhead. Day and night he thought about becoming red, and how beautiful he would look then, and how people would admire him, and he began to fret and worry more and more each day, for fear he should miss Mother Nature.

Again and again he asked the Staghorn when she would come, and each time the Staghorn told him the same thing,— "In the autumn."

But at last the Staghorn grew tired of always being asked the same question, and refused to answer. Then the Leaf asked, "When does autumn came?" and the Staghorn replied, "At the end of summer."

"Is it nearly the end of the summer yet?" asked the Leaf.

"No; I'm very glad to say it is not," replied the Staghorn, rather sharply, for he wanted to be quiet and enjoy the breeze and sunshine, and the Leaf disturbed his peace with his continual questions.

"Don't you long for the autumn?" asked the Leaf.

"No!" answered the Staghorn, curtly.

Then the Leaf saw that the Staghorn did not want to talk any more, so he left off asking questions for a while.

But though he did not speak about the autumn, he did not for a moment forget it. As the days passed, he became more and more anxious to see Mother Nature, and ask her to paint him red; and he spent his time in imagining how fine he would look on a table, for the Americans said they put their red and yellow leaves in vases. He thought it would be much grander to live in a vase than on a tree; and he was so excited at the idea that he did not bother to take his food properly, and he did not eat the sweet juices of his mother tree or drink in the fresh rains and dews. And so he began to grow pale, and to lose his bright green colour, and he felt strangely tired. Then, as the days passed, he grew more and more dissatisfied, until at last there really was not a more discontented leaf in the whole of the bush.

The weather had been intensely hot, and the trees and ferns were all feeling tired, and wishing for the cooler days. Out of the ground rose moist, warm vapours, which made everything feel sticky and damp. Then one night the weather suddenly changed, and there was a fresh, cool feeling in the breeze.

The old Staghorn looked up to the Leaf as soon as it was light, and said—"Autumn has come."

The Leaf trembled with excitement as he said eagerly, "Has it, really? And will Mother Nature soon come now?"

"Yes," replied the Staghorn. "She should be here to-day."

The Leaf was too excited to speak, and he just sat and shook on his twig. Then he heard the Staghorn say in a surprised, eager tone, "Why, here she comes now!"

The Leaf turned to where the Staghorn was pointing, and there, coming through themselves, was a tall and beautiful woman. Her eyes were bright and brown, and her hair was the colour of ripe corn. She wore a ruddy brown gown, the colour of a russet apple, and in her hand she carried a golden pail filled with a red and yellow mixture.

"She is robed in her autumn clothes," said the Staghorn; "and has the paint in her pail. She must be going to begin to-day."

Even as he spoke, Mother Nature stopped before a tall gum tree, and, stretching up her arm, put a splash of colour on some leaves. The Leaf saw that they at once lost their blue shade, and became a light yellow. Then Mother Nature came along towards the Leaf, touching branches here and there as she passed, and leaving a red or yellow spot of colour wherever her brush had rested. At last she reached the Leaf's tree, looked at it for a second, and was just going to pass by, when she heard a voice say—

"Please don't go. Won't you paint me, too?"

She looked round in surprise, and saw the Leaf gazing anxiously at her as he repeated—"Please, please paint me, too!"

"Oh, no, dear. I couldn't paint you," said Mother Nature, kindly. "You are too young."

"Ah, no, I'm not. I'm quite grown up, and I do want to be painted red."

"But why, my child?"

"Because red leaves are the most beautiful, and people put them into vases, and I want to live in a vase, and—"

The Leaf stopped for breath, and Mother Nature replied, sadly, "Ah, yes, red leaves are indeed beautiful, but a leaf must suffer very much before it becomes red, and then it often lies on the ground for days before it is picked up and put into a vase."

"I don't mind how much I suffer, or if I do have to lie on the ground. I'm not afraid of pain. Oh, if only I could be red!"

"But you are too young to suffer, my child."

"No, no, I'm not. I don't mind how you hurt me, if only you will paint me red. Oh, please say you will," and the Leaf stretched eagerly out and touched her hand.

Mother Nature smiled sadly, as she answered:

"Very well, my child. Since you long so much to be red,

you shall have your wish. But I hope you won't be sorry afterwards."

"Oh, no; I'll only be happy," cried the Leaf. "I'm not a bit frightened of pain."

Then Mother Nature dipped her brush into her pail, and splashed it right into the Leaf's face.

For a moment he felt as if he were choking, and he could not see. All through his body fire seemed to be rushing, and the pain was terrific.

"Oh, oh, oh!" he cried, and turned to Mother Nature to ask her to take away this terrible feeling. But when he was able to clear the paint from his eyes, so that he could see, she was out of sight. He bent as far forward as he could, but it was no use. She had vanished.

After a little while the pain grew less, and he thought to himself, "Oh, well; I'll soon be all right. I am changing colour already, and I expect by the time I am quite red, I shall be perfectly well again."

But each day, instead of feeling better, he seemed to become weaker and weaker. He no longer felt as if fire was rushing through his veins, but as if all his blood was ebbing away. He was strangely drowsy, too, and wanted to sleep all the time. He took no notice of the birds that flew above his head, and he didn't answer when his old friend the Staghorn spoke to him. He didn't even seem to mind whether he was red or not. All he wanted to do was to sleep.

One day, as he was feeling more than usually drowsy, he was suddenly awakened by voices beneath him, and, as he looked round, he saw a girl pointing to him, and heard her say—"What a pretty red leaf!"

In an instant he was wide awake. He forgot to be tired;

forgot he was ill—all he thought of was that at last he was red. At last he would be carried into a house, and live in a vase and decorate a table. Oh, how happy he was! He jumped with joy, and in a moment he had shaken himself free from his twig, and was floating through the air.

Softly and slowly he sank till he reached the earth at the girl's feet.

He lay there trembling with excitement, waiting for her to pick him up and carry him to her house. But he waited in vain, for the girl was gazing at the old Staghorn, and had quite forgotten the Leaf, and though he lay quite close to her foot, she did not notice him, and in a little while she walked on, leaving him alone.

The Leaf could not understand it at all. He did not want to lie on the ground; he wanted to live in a vase, but he did not know how he was to reach one. He knew people put red leaves in vases, and yet this girl had not taken him.

There he lay, however, all that night, and all the next day, but no one else passed him. All round him other leaves were lying, but they were a queer brown colour, which the Leaf had never seen before; and they rustled in a strange manner, and when the Leaf spoke to them they did not answer. They were poor dead leaves, but he did not know that, and thought they were unkind not to speak to him.

As the second day passed into night, he felt very sad and lonely, and he wished he was back on the tree with his brothers. The old Staghorn was ever so high above his head, too far to hear him, and the maiden-hair ferns which were close by were whispering to themselves all the time, and took no notice of him; so there was no one at all for the Leaf to talk to, and he was very miserable.

Then, just as the sun was sinking behind the Sassafras trees, he heard a gentle rustling, and, turning, he saw Mother Nature walking towards him.

"Oh, dear Mother Nature," he cried, "take me home to my branch. I don't like being on the ground, and I am so miserable."

"You shouldn't be miserable," said Mother Nature. "You are now a most lovely red leaf, and if you wait long enough, perhaps someone will pick you up and put you into a vase."

"I don't want to be in a vase. I only want to be back on my tree. Dear Mother Nature, take me back!"

But Mother Nature shook her head, and answered sadly—

"There is no going back, my child. You wanted to be red, and you said you did not mind pain. You have had your own way, and I cannot alter things now. If you had been content to remain green, you would have lived on your tree for years. I did not want to paint you, and tried to persuade you to stay green; but you would not be happy until I touched you with my paint brush, so I did as you asked."

The poor Leaf grew sadder and sadder as she spoke, and when she had ceased, he felt a strange cold shiver strike through his veins, and he cried—"Oh, if only I had been satisfied!"

But before he could say another word, he rolled over lifeless, and there he lay, a sad, dead Leaf.

Then Mother Nature, with tears in her eyes, took a handful of soft warm earth, and placed it over him.

THE STORY OF THE TURPENTINES

THE TURPENTINES were the saddest trees in the forest. All the other trees spent their lives happily dancing with the wind and gossiping cheerfully to each other, but the Turpentines were stiff and silent, and never danced and enjoyed life. And the reason of their sadness was that they thought nobody wanted them, or cared anything about them. Poets wrote songs about the gums and the wattles, and painters made pictures of them, but no one ever painted or sang about the Turpentines, while men who came to the forest to cut the big trees for timber, would walk past them without even a glance, and would pass on to where the big gums grew.

Perhaps the Turpentines should have been glad that the woodcutters did not chop them down and carry them away. But they were not. They knew that the logs taken away from the bush were all used for some purpose or other, and that was what they wanted most of all—to be useful.

At night, when all the woodcutters had gone home and the birds were sleeping, the trees would whisper to each other and talk about their brothers who had been carried away by men. The wind used to bring them tidings of the absent ones, and they would talk with deep interest of the wonderful things that the travellers were doing.

"I hear that my brothers are welcomed everywhere when great strength is needed," said the Iron Bark, "and they send them to all parts of the world to build wharves and bridges."

"My brothers are also much sought after," said the Tallow Wood, "they help to make railways and houses, and all things that men use most."

"Not all things," said the Spotted Gum. "Your brothers are no use for making carriages and coaches. That is where our family excel. I think we may truthfully be called the most travelled of all trees, for we are not only used for carriages and carts, but we often go to sea in the decks of ships and journey across the ocean."

"It's a pity you don't stop in one place as decent woods should," growled the Brush Box, who was sulky because his family never travelled, but were made into blocks to pave the streets.

"It wouldn't do for us all to be such slow-coaches as you are," replied the Spotted Gum saucily.

"Well, well," interrupted the Iron Bark, who hated a quarrel. "We are all useful in our own way, and I really don't know what men would do without any of us."

"Except us," said the Turpentines sadly. "They don't want us. We are of no use for anything."

"That's because you crack up directly you are cut," said the Spotted Gum, "why don't you behave better?"

"It's because we get so excited," said the Turpentines plaintively. "We would calm down and get cool afterwards, but men are always in such a hurry, and won't wait for us to recover."

"You shouldn't be so silly," said the Spotted Gum, who was conceited and gave himself airs ever since one of his brothers had become a pair of wheels for the King's carriage.

"We know it's silly," said the Turpentines, "but we can't help being nervous."

"The Spotted Gum laughed with good-natured contempt. "Silly old things," he said: "but I suppose, when one hasn't travelled one cannot help being stupid and awkward. Travel broadens one's experience."

"Broadens one's impudence, I should say," muttered the Brush Box.

"There, there," interrupted the Iron Bark. "We can't all be used for the same things at the same time. Perhaps your turn will come soon," he added, turning to the Turpentines.

"Perhaps it will," agreed the Turpentines, rather hopelessly, though they looked at the Iron Bark with gratitude for his kind words.

The years passed by, and each season found fewer and fewer trees in the bush. Men came with axes and saws and cut them down; then horses came and dragged them away out of sight, and they were seen no more in the bush. One by one the Turpentines' companions were taken away, till there were very few left. Even the smaller trees, the Silky Oaks and the Red Beans, were carried off and used for furniture, but the Turpentines remained untouched. The wind brought great tales back to the survivors of doings in many lands, and every year the Turpentines grew more and more hopeless of ever being useful. And the sap within them, which had been sweet and pure, gradually became heavy and bitter, and the trees themselves were not as patient and good-natured as they had been. They would listen enviously to the tales of the other trees, and wonder why they should be so unlucky.

"What have we done to be punished in this way," they

said one day to their friend the Iron Bark. "Why should all the other trees be used and not us?"

"Your time will come," said the Iron Bark soothingly, "I feel sure that you will go away from here some day and be used for something. Perhaps then you will wish yourselves back in the calm old bush again," he added with a sigh.

"That's not very likely," cried the Turpentines. "If we could only go out into the world and be of use, we would never want to come back here again."

"Ah, they all think that, but many of them grow homesick, and long for a sight of the dear old bush. Some of them have many troubles to fight against. I have just had some very sad news about some of my own brothers."

"We are very sorry to hear that," said the Turpentines sympathetically. "Is it any of the family that we know.?"

"Yes, you knew them. Do you remember that family that lived just over the rise?"

"Yes, yes, the biggest and strongest of all."

"Yes, they were all splendidly grown, and looked fit for any work, didn't they?"

"Indeed they did."

"Well, that is what men thought too, and they took them away across the world to build a wharf for the King. It was to be the best and strongest wharf in the kingdom, and my brothers were chosen to be the piles to support all the rest. For some years they did all that was required of them, but now I hear that the little insects that live in the water there have bitten into them, and they are all weak and ill, and quite unfit for work, and they are to be thrown away as useless."

"That is very sad, very sad, indeed," murmured the Turpentines. Then one said, "But they must have enjoyed themselves while they were well!"

"They did. They used to send me word of how they liked it, and of what fun they had with the little waves and fishes. And they used to have great fights with the big waves sometimes, for the sea would try to wash them away. But they always conquered and remained in their places."

"It must be glorious to fight with the big waves," said one Turpentine.

"Oh, I wish I could have the chance!" said another.

"It is dreadful to think," went on the Iron Bark, "That trees that were strong enough to withstand the waves should be eaten into and made ill by tiny little insects."

"They wouldn't bite us," cried a young Turpentine. "'We're too bitter inside."

"Oh, I wish the wharf-builders would try us," cried another.

"Perhaps they will now," said the Iron Bark, for there are no more of my brothers big enough to go, and no other trees are strong enough."

"If only they would!" sighed the Turpentines. "We would show them that we are to be trusted."

The very next day two men came to the bush, and to the amazement of all, stopped before the Turpentines.

"They are magnificent trees, and I am quite confident that they will be the very thing we want," said one.

"I quite agree with you," said the other, "and I think it has been a great mistake not using them before."

Then they measured the girths, and after marking quite a number of trees, went away.

The Turpentines could hardly speak for excitement, as they called to the Iron Bark—"What are they going to do?

Are they going to send us away?"

"It looks very like it," said the Iron Bark, "but you will soon know."

The next morning men came with axes and saws and began to chop down the biggest Turpentine. They talked as they worked, and one man said he thought it waste of time chopping such rubbish.

"They always split as soon as they are cut," he said. "The master says that they heal up again when they are put into water," said the other.

"Are these going into the water?"

"Yes, I believe they are going to be sent across the world to make piles for a wharf."

At these words the Turpentines could not contain their joy, and they laughed and jumped with happiness in a way they had never done before.

"Hurrah!" they shouted. "At last we are going to be of use in the world."

"I told you your time would come," said the Iron Bark, who was himself as pleased as the Turpentines. "You will soon leave the bush for ever."

In a few weeks all the big Turpentines had been cut. Then horses came and dragged them away.

"Good-bye!" cried the Iron Bark, "and good luck go with you."

"Good-bye, good-bye," cried the Turpentines, "we will never forget you." And then they were dragged down the hill and away from the bush for ever.

They travelled across the country for some time, till they reached the river. Here they found small sailing ships, which the men called ketches. The Turpentines were put on to the decks of these ketches, two on each; the men hoisted sail, and the boats began to move away.

"Isn't this fine?" the trees called to each other. "This is really seeing life at last."

As they sailed down the river, the smell of the sea came floating towards them, and the waves splashed their spray on to the decks, and the Turpentines enjoyed it thoroughly.

The river broadened as they neared the sea, till at last they came to an open harbour with a big city on its shores. Here there were many ships, of all sorts and sizes. The Turpentines were landed on the wharf close to a large sailing ship with three tall masts, which they heard the men say was to take them across the ocean. They heard that they were to go "'tween decks," and they were greatly puzzled as to how they were to get there, for the hole which led from the upper deck was only large enough for a man, and there seemed no possibility of a tall tree being put through it.

However, they did not worry, for they had found already that when these men said they were going to do a thing they were always able to do it. So the Turpentines just waited to see what would happen.

Early next morning they saw two sailors working on a little bridge hanging from the side of the ship; the trees watched with interest, and by and by they saw the men lift one of the plates from the bows of the ship, then another and another, till there was a hole quite big enough for the largest tree to go through.

Then the wharf labourers came and set some machinery going; big hooks came down and lifted one of the Turpentines up into the air, and out across the water till the end of the trunk came into line with the hole in the ship. Then slowly it was pushed forward, and bit by bit disappeared into the ship. One by one all the trees were treated in the same way and, at the end of a few weeks, they were lying side by side in the ship's hold, and the hole in the bows was closed up again.

Then off once more they went on their travels. It was very dark in their resting-place, but the trees were too excited to mind, and they talked and wondered about what was to happen next. Outside they could hear the waves running by, and sometimes they would hear their old friend the wind whistling past, and they knew he would take news of them to their comrades in the bush.

Weeks and weeks passed in this way, and at last the ship came to her destination. The rolling stopped; once again the plates were removed from the bows, and the sunlight streamed in on the Turpentines. And very glad they were to see it, too, for they were beginning to grow weary of the darkness.

Soon men came with strong chains and hooks, and one by one the trees were moved on to the land. They looked round with great excitement and curiosity to see where they were, and found a country different from any they had known before. Green grassy slopes ran down to the sea, with here and there shady trees of a brighter, lighter colour than the trees of the old bush. But though the grass and trees were brighter, the sky and sea were not so blue, and the sun was not so warm as in their own land. For a moment a feeling of homesickness swept through the Turpentines, and they longed for the sight of the rough old Iron Bark, and their little brothers.

Then a familiar voice said—"Well, old friends, you have

travelled a long way," and there was the wind, kissing them in an affectionate greeting.

"You ought to be very happy here," he said, when he had kissed them all, "for you are going to be very useful."

"Are we?" cried the Turpentines eagerly, quite forgetting their homesickness, "what are we going to do?"

"Well," said the wind, "I have heard that you are going to make the piles for the King's own wharf."

"The King's own wharf!" echoed the Turpentines. "Oh, that couldn't be true."

"I only tell you what I hear," replied the wind. "And now I must be off, for those fishing boats are waiting for me," and away he blew.

"The King's own wharf!" repeated the Turpentines to each other. "Oh, if it should be true! We should be the happiest trees in all the world. But it can't be true, for it is always the best Iron Barks that are used for that. No, it can't possibly be true."

But it was true. The next day an odd-looking boat came up with a tall scaffolding on it, and a strong pulley. One after the other the Turpentines were lifted high up into the air, then plunged deep down into the water till they touched the bottom. Then a heavy hammer came down thud, thud, thud on their heads, driving them deeper and deeper into the sand, till there was only about a quarter of their length above water. The hammering hurt them dreadfully at first, but the cool, clean salt water soon cooled and healed them, and by the time the rest of the wharf was built, they were all as well and healthy as they had ever been.

When they had been in the water a few days, swarms of little insects came and tried to bite them. But the Turpentines grew so angry at the thought of these little creatures trying to harm them when they were the mainstays of the King's own wharf, that all their sap grew sour with indignation; and the insects, finding that the Turpentines were not sweet to taste, swam away to feed elsewhere, leaving the trees whole and unharmed.

Then at last came the opening day, and the wharf was gaily decorated with flags, and bands played loudly. Presently they began to play a tune that the Turpentines had heard far away in their own land. They could not tell why, but it filled them with excitement. Then came cheers and shouting, and in a few minutes a white yacht sailed up to the wharf. As the boat stopped, there was still more shouting, and then a plank was laid down, and the Turpentines saw the King walk from the yacht on to the wharf.

The King walked up and down the wharf with the master builder, looking with interest at every detail, and the Turpentines heard him praise the rails and the floor and the shape of the wharf. Then he walked towards the oldest Turpentine, which was at the end of the wharf, and putting his hand against it, said—"These are very fine piles you have."

"Yes, your Majesty, they are the finest we could get. They are Turpentines from Australia."

"Ah," said the King, "there are no trees in my kingdom so useful for piles as the Turpentines from Australia." Then he passed on.

But down in the water below were the happiest trees in the world. For the Turpentines that had once been despised and passed by as worthless, had become the most honoured and useful trees in the King's whole kingdom.

THE GALLANT GUM TREES

THE TREES in the gully grew green and thick, for the stream that ran and danced all day over the rocks brought them nourishing food, which made them strong. The hot winds never blew on them, and the sun only sent his kindest rays upon them. So it came about that the Tree-ferns and Wattles, the Myrtles and Sassafras, which grew along the banks of the stream, were always cool and green and shady, and the most admired in the district.

Up on the hill-side where the young Gums grew, things were very different. The loose sandy soil in which their roots were embedded contained very little food for them, for all the water used to run down the hill to the stream in the gully. For this reason the Wattles and Myrtles got most of the Gum-trees' food as well as their own. But the Gums never grumbled. Of all the trees in the forest they were the bravest and most cheerful. When the hot winds blew and scorched their faces, they would laugh merrily together, and say: "No need of overcoats to-day!" When the cold wintry blasts came tearing down from the mountain, they would dance and wave their arms, shouting to each other, "Fine, fresh weather, isn't it? Makes one want to dance."

If the rain poured in torrents for days together they would gladly drink in all they could, saying: "There's nothing like a good shower bath for making you big and strong." And if the drought came and dried up all the moisture in the soil, so that there was scarcely any nourishment for them, they would hold up their heads and say—"We believe in fasting sometimes, it keeps us slim and graceful."

So, whatever the weather, the Gums were contented, and enjoyed their lives to the utmost. Because they were so happy everyone loved them, and the birds and bees would play amongst their leaves and make their homes in their branches; the native bears and opossums would climb their trunks, and feed on their leaves; and insects would hide under their bark for protection. The Gum trees loved them all and were glad to be of so much use in the world.

Indeed, there were very few things that they did not love, but the ones they cared for most of all were the green trees in the gully. They knew that everyone admired the gully-trees, but they were never hurt nor jealous; indeed they were as proud of the greenness and luxuriance of the gully-trees as if they themselves had made them.

"Look at those Tree-ferns," they would say, "did you ever see anything so cool and fresh?" Or they would ask—"Could there be anything more beautiful and graceful than those Wattles and Myrtles?" and they would honestly wonder why the birds and bees ever came near them, when they could live amongst the trees in the gully. For they were quite unaware of their own charm and sweetness, and really believed that they were not worth looking at.

And the gully-trees agreed with them on that point. They were so used to being admired by everyone that they thought themselves the most beautiful things in the world, and even took it as a matter of course that the Gums should think so too. They were fond of the Gums, but in a very patronising way, and would laugh at them for being tall and scraggy instead of round and thick like themselves. The Gums laughed too, and so they were all good friends.

The gully-trees never thought of being grateful to the Gums for the shelter and protection they gave them from sun and wind, and the Gums never dreamed of being offended because the gullytrees took more than their own share of food.

They thus lived on quietly and contentedly for many years, watching the seasons come and go each with its own treasure. Then one day a very bad-tempered Summer arrived. She came very early, before Spring had left the land, and as she arrived in a fury, the gentler season fled before her. Scorching winds and blazing sunbeams followed in her train, and before many days were past the whole land was suffering from her cruelty. The smaller plants and flowers were shrivelled as though by a furnace; the young birds, unable to escape to cooler regions, dropped and died; even the big trees grew faint and weary, and bent their heads before her.

In the farms and orchards men went about with worried looks, for the young crops and fruit were being killed, and famine stared them in the face.

Down in the gully the trees moaned and sighed with pain, for they had never known such heat, and they cried to the Gums to try and shelter them. Up on the hill the heat was worst of all, and some of the younger Gums were beginning to moan, but their bigger brothers still talked cheerfully to each other, and tried to keep up the spirits of the weaker ones. When they heard the cries of the gully-trees, they were saddened, for it was beyond their power to protect them from the fiery blasts.

"Help us, oh, help us if you love us!" cried the gully-trees.

The Gums bent gently towards them and answered sadly, "We would give our lives to save you, you dear, beautiful things, but we are powerless."

The cruel Summer heard these words, and laughed mockingly.

"You would give your lives for them, would you?" she said with a sneer. "You will soon have a chance to do so." So saying, she raced away across the mountain.

That very night the chance came. The Sun went down a fiery ball behind the hills, and, as he disappeared, a red glow was seen to rise in the eastern sky.

"Is the Sun coming back again already?" asked a baby tree, in tears.

The bigger Gums shook their heads. "It is not the Sun," they said; "it is a greater enemy than he. It is the Fire."

At these words there rose from all the trees and bushes a wail of despair, for the Fire is the most dreaded of all enemies. Down in the gully the trees shook and trembled with terror.

"Is it coming this way?" they cried, for they could not see the red glow yet.

"It is coming this way, and coming quickly," answered the Gums gravely. "Oh, what shall we do, what shall we do?" sobbed the gully-trees. "We shall all be killed!"

Their cries were drowned by a howl from the Summer winds, and at that instant the Fire appeared on the top of the opposite hill. With red hair flying and blue arms waving it leaped from tree to tree, licking up everything before it. Behind it came the hot winds, driving it forward and laughing fiendishly at their work.

Already the Gums on the hill-side could feel the breath of the flames, but though their faces were almost scorched, the sap ran cool and calm within them. Flocks of birds came screeching towards them, and flew rapidly past, together with a troop of bush animals, all crying aloud, "The Fire, the Fire!"

The gully-trees heard them, and wept piteously in their terror.

The sound of their friends' grief and terror roused a feeling in the heart of the Gums that they had never known before. It was their fighting instinct. Instantly they decided to fight to the death to save their darlings in the gully. They lifted their heads and waved their arms in defiance at the Fire, shouting in one voice—"Come and fight us if you dare!"

The Fire heard the challenge, and with a roar leaped right across the gully, over the gully-trees, and hurled its flames into the midst of the Gums. Fiercely the battle raged, the Gums dashing their green leaves into the face of the flames. But the Fire was stronger, and very soon the trees were overwhelmed and conquered. Then the Fire passed on, leaving the gully-trees all green and untouched; but on the hill-side stood a defeated army of burnt black trunks, where so short a time before the brave young Gums had dared the foe.

. . . .

In a few days the Fire had burnt itself out, and then the rain sent soft showers that cooled and refreshed the parched and burnt-up earth. After the rain had washed away all the black stains and dust, the gully-trees were as green and beautiful as they had ever been, and no one could tell by looking at them that they had so nearly perished in the flames. But the gully-trees themselves knew the danger they had escaped. They had no chance of forgetting their peril, for there before their eyes were the black trunks of the Gums which had saved them. And they did not laugh happily as of yore, but drooped their heads and mourned for their lost friends.

"It does not seem right that we should be as strong and healthy as ever, while our poor friends are all dead," said the Sassafras tree sadly.

"To think that we will never see their happy faces nodding to us again!" sighed the Wattle.

"Nor hear their merry voices calling to each other," said the Myrtle.

"Life will be very lonely without them," said the Tree-fern, "and I wish we had never laughed at them."

At this there was silence, for all the trees felt sad and ashamed to think that they had ever laughed at their brave friends on the hill-side.

The silence was broken by a tiny whisper which seemed to come from the ground, and which said—"Don't grieve, dear trees, we shall meet again."

The trees looked at each other in astonishment.

"What is it?" they asked each other. "It sounds like the voices of the Gum-trees."

"It is the spirit of the Gums," cried the Stream, who had heard all the conversation. "Listen, listen, and you will hear it again."

The trees all bent eagerly towards the ground, and again

the soft voice spoke.

"We are not dead," it said, "though we are badly wounded. But our sap is still fresh and cool, and we will be ourselves again some day."

The trees could not keep still with excitement. Their leaves rustled and quivered with joy, and they asked, all together, "Oh, is it true, is it true?"

"Yes," called the Stream, as he danced along, "it is quite true. Before many seasons have passed your friends will be the same as ever. Fire cannot kill their brave hearts, and while a tree's heart is alive, it cannot die."

"Hurrah! hurrah!" shouted all the gully-trees, as they waved their arms with joy.

"Hurrah! hurrah!" cried the birds also, when they heard the cheering, and flew away to spread the news to the 'Possums and Native Bears.

And little by little the Gums began to recover and put forth little shoots to show that their wounds were healing. The kind rain sent showers which washed all the burnt leaves into the earth and gave the Gums fresh food, which strengthened them. When the Summer arrived again she was in a good temper and sorry for all the harm she had done; so she brought only gentle sunbeams and refreshing winds with her; and everything helped the Gums to recover.

At the end of a few seasons, all the earth had recovered from the fire. The flowers and small plants covered the ground more gaily than ever; the crops and fruit were bigger and more plentiful than they had ever been before, and on the hillside the Gum-trees waved and sang quite merrily.

But a great change had come over them. Instead of the ragged, straggling things of dull green they had been before, there rose tier after tier of straight, strong trees, all thickly clothed with leaves of a glorious copper colour, which gleamed and glistened in the sunshine, and made the hillside glow like burnished armour.

And no longer were the gully-trees the most admired, for everyone stopped to gaze at the hill-side and say: "Oh, what beautiful Gum-trees!"

The gully-trees themselves admired their friends more than anyone, and were never tired of telling them how lovely they were.

As for the Gums, they laughed and enjoyed life just in the same old way, and answered all the compliments by saying: "After all, it doesn't matter much what your face is like, if only your sap keeps cool and pure. Sap is the thing that counts!"

www.ingramcontent.com/pod-product-compliance
Lightning Source LLC
Chambersburg PA
CBHW031109080526
44587CB00011B/897